Hostas

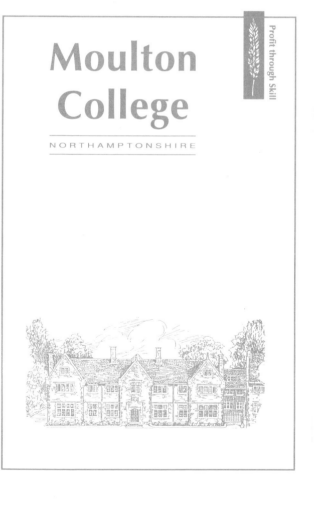

Moulton College

NORTHAMPTONSHIRE

Profit through Skill

RHS WISLEY HANDBOOKS

Hostas

Diana Grenfell

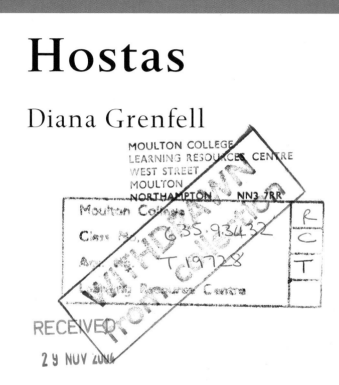
CASSELL ILLUSTRATED

THE ROYAL HORTICULTURAL SOCIETY

The right of Diana Grenfell to be identified as the author of
this work has been asserted by her in accordance with the
Copyright, Designs and Patents Act 1988.

First published in Great Britain in 2002 by
Cassell Illustrated
Octopus Publishing Group
2–4 Heron Quays, London E14 4PJ

A CIP catalogue record for this book is available
from the British Library
ISBN 0-304-36288-3

Designer: Justin Hunt
Commissioning Editor: Camilla Stoddart

Printed in Slovenia by DELO tiskarna
by arrangement with Preševrnova družba

Contents

Title page: Hosta
'Stiletto' is a small,
spreading hosta best
grown in a border or
light woodland.

Introduction

Hostas are the most popular foliage plants in both Britain and America. Their popularity arises from the sheer sumptuousness of their leaves. Many varieties of hostas have leaves that are large, heart-shaped and strongly textured, building up into overlapping mounds of blue, yellow or green, often with the margins or the centres of the leaves white, cream or yellow. Other hostas have smaller, more graceful, often lance-shaped leaves. Most types produce short spires of trumpet or bell-shaped flowers in shades of mauve or lilac, but a few are pure white, though not many are grown for their flowers alone.

Botanists recognize some 40–70 wild species of *Hosta* and breeders working with this essentially simple palette have created something in excess of 4,000 garden varieties, in almost every conceivable size, shape and colour combination. Over 850 of these garden varieties are listed in the *RHS Plant Finder*.

Hostas may seem to be very modern plants, but their story goes back a long way. They are all natives of the Far East, particularly Japan, China and Korea and have been cultivated in Japanese gardens and temples for literally hundreds of years. In the West, nothing was known of hostas until the early seventeenth century when Engelbert Kaempfer, a medical doctor with the Dutch East India Company stationed in Japan, made a drawing of the plant we now know as *Hosta lancifolia*. The first hosta to actually reach the West was a Chinese species, *H. plantaginea*, whose seed was sent by the French consul in Macao to the Jardin de Plantes in Paris sometime between

A pleasing combination of huge leaved hostas, 'Sum and Substance' (background) and 'Gray Cole' (foreground), punctuated with the small leaved Lamium galeobdolen, fills a shaded corner.

1784 and 1789. *H. plantaginea* is quite distinct among hostas in having extraordinarily long, 13cm (5in), white, trumpet-shaped flowers, with an exquisite fragrance. A native of southern China, it was thought to be frost tender and was originally grown in stove houses, which were hot and humid glasshouses with atmospheres like tropical jungles. Another Chinese species, *H. ventricosa*, was introduced to the West soon after *H. plantaginea*.

The first main importation of hostas to the West was in 1830 when Philipp von Siebold, another medical doctor with the Dutch East India company in Japan, shipped a collection of hostas to Ghent in Belgium. They were then grown on in the Siebold nursery in Leiden, Holland. From there they were distributed to Britain and to other countries in Europe. The first hostas to reach North America were almost certainly imported from Europe, and were probably mainly the Siebold plants mentioned above. *The American Flower Garden Directory* of 1839 lists three varieties, and Rand's *Garden Flowers* published in 1866 lists six varieties, all of which were already in cultivation in Europe.

The first major importation of hostas to America direct from Japan was by Thomas Hogg junior, whose father Thomas Hogg senior, had trained as a nurseryman in London. Thomas junior was made a United States Marshal by President Lincoln, who sent him to Japan in 1862. This makes him one of the earliest Americans to have travelled to Japan, and to have collected plants there. He sent consignments of plants back to the Thomas Hogg nursery in Manhattan. There is no specific record of his sending back hostas, but it is known that he bought them, particularly variegated ones, from Japanese street markets, and that at some point he took at least two of these to America. Both of these, the hostas now known as *Hosta undulata* var. *albomarginata* and *H. decorata* 'Decorata', have green leaves with white margins and would have been called *fukurin fu giboshi* in Japanese, which means 'the green leaf hosta with variegated edge'. Since westerners generally have difficulties with Japanese names, these hostas quickly became known as Thomas Hogg's hostas or *Hosta* 'Thomas Hogg'.

WILD HABITATS OF HOSTAS

When hostas were first introduced to the West, botanists generally assumed that they had been collected in the wild and were wild species. However, it was subsequently realized, that many of these early introductions, some of which had variegated foliage (for example *Hosta undulata*) had come from gardens, and were therefore cultivated varieties rather than wild species. (Although variegated plants do occur in the wild, they are rare and seldom survive for long, lacking the vigour to compete with normal green-leaved plants.) In the UK, the status of these so-called species has been down-graded to 'species of convenience', although their specific names are still expressed in italic type as if they were true species, for example *H. lancifolia* and *H. undulata*. In the USA, they are regarded as cultivated varieties or 'specioids', and their names are expressed in Roman type inside single quotation marks, for example 'Lancifolia'. This particular plant has long been known to be a sterile hybrid.

9

The wild species of hostas are typically clump-forming perennial plants with green leaves and usually mauve, bell- or funnel-shaped flowers borne above the foliage on short, upright stems. In common with other plants, the leaves of wild populations can vary on account of regional or temperature differences, which sometimes makes identification difficult. The commonest wild hosta in Japan, *H. montana*, grows at the edges of forests and in forest glades, and this is regarded as the typical wild habitat of hostas, and in gardens they are generally grown as woodland or shade-loving plants. Several more unusual species, however, have adapted themselves to quite different conditions. *H. longissima,* which has long and narrow, almost grassy leaves, grows in damp meadows at high altitude where its leaves are shaded by the leaves and stems of grasses and the meadows are often covered by low clouds, while the white-backed *H. hypoleuca* normally grows in full sun clinging to precipitous, south-facing volcanic cliffs. In such conditions, it usually only produces one huge leaf, the back of which is covered in a fine white powder to protect it from the heat reflected by the bare rocks. The diminutive *H. venusta*, with leaves no bigger than a thumb-nail, grows as an epiphyte on mossy tree trunks, and *H. kiosumiensis* grows on rocks or tree roots at the edges of streams, its white roots trailing in the water. Some of these more unusual species can be difficult to cultivate in gardens.

The diminutive species, Hosta venusta, *makes a neat clump in the rock garden and peat bed, or planted as a contrast with a large-leaved hosta.*

CULTIVATED VARIETIES AND HYBRIDS

Nowadays, few of the green-leaved wild hostas are grown in the garden, having been ousted by the cultivated varieties and hybrids with coloured or variegated leaves. Long before hostas reached the West, Japanese gardeners had started to select forms with white- or yellow-variegated leaves. Such plants arise either as seedlings or as sports; sports are side-shoots, exhibiting some variation arising on an otherwise normal plant. Many of the hostas to reach Ghent in Siebold's original introduction from Japan were of these variegated sorts. Nothing quite like them had been seen in Europe until then.

Since those early days, when only a handful of hostas were known, their numbers have increased dramatically. Some 4,000 varieties have been named worldwide, although the International Registration Authority for Hostas in the United States lists less than half this number. Until quite recently, these new varieties originated as seedlings or sports, but the modern trend is for new varieties to arise in tissue culture, which is the laboratory technique by which plants are mass-produced from single cells grown in nutrient jelly in test-tubes.

THE NAMING OF HOSTAS

The correct naming of hostas has been a problem ever since they first became known in the West, as no formalized system existed before their arrival. The Chinese and Japanese had their own systems for naming plants, both vulgar and scholarly, but in the West, the plants were simply given descriptions that served as names. The first hosta illustrated by Engelbert Kaempfer was called '*Joksan, vulgo gibboosi Gladiolus Plantaginis folio*', which translates as 'the Joksan commonly known as gibboosi; the gladiolus with the plantain-like leaves'. 'Gibboosi' or 'giboshi' is the Japanese name for a hosta, and to this day hostas are still known, if only occasionally, as plantain lilies (from the fancied resemblance of their leaves to those of plantains).

With the adoption of the Linnaean binomial system, confusion multiplied at first as various botanists assigned different species to different genera. For a while, *Hosta ventricosa* was known as *Hemerocallis caerulea*, which by today's standards would make it a daylily. The name *Hosta* was first used in 1812 to honour the Austrian botanist Nicholas Thomas Host (1761–1834), who was the author of a flora of Austria; the name fell into disuse, however, and *Funkia* was used in its place. *Funkia* honoured Heinrich Christian Funk, a botanist of whom little is known, and the name was commonly used for hostas by Gertrude Jekyll and gardeners of her generation; it is still widely used as a common name for hostas in much of continental Europe. Today, the correct naming of plants is governed by two codes: the International Code of Nomenclature of Cultivated Plants and the International Code of Botanical Nomenclature. Under these, the name *Hosta* has been determined as the correct name for the genus.

The position of hostas in the plant kingdom has also been a matter for debate. Plainly, they are monocotyledonous plants because they only produce one cotyledon or seed-leaf when the seeds germinate. Within this group, hostas were placed for a long time in the lily family, Liliaceae, but this was not satisfactory because Liliaceae was too large a family, and too ill-defined. Under a new system of classification, originally devised by R.M.T. Dahlgren, H.T. Clifford and P.F. Yeo in 1985, and adopted by the Royal Botanic Gardens, Kew in 1987, it is widely, but not universally, accepted that hostas belong in their own family, the *Hostaceae*. Taxonomy, which is the study of the classification of plants, is not an exact science and opinions still differ.

The only absolute way of identifying a hosta species and its cultivated forms is by its flowers since leaves may vary with cultural conditions or depart from the norm by being variegated. The flowers of any one species will always be the same. With modern hybrid hostas, which often have complex parentage and usually bell-shaped flowers, there may be no absolute way of being certain. However, keen growers and collectors of hostas can often tell which garden variety is which from its general colouring and deportment.

THE FOLIAGE OF HOSTAS

Hostas are frost-hardy, clump-forming perennials with fleshy white roots. They usually form dense mounds of large,

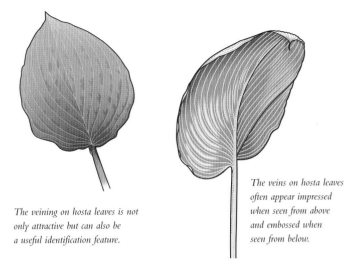

The veining on hosta leaves is not only attractive but can also be a useful identification feature.

The veins on hosta leaves often appear impressed when seen from above and embossed when seen from below.

heart-shaped, strongly textured and overlapping leaves, which spring directly from the roots, although in some varieties leaves also occur on the flower stems. The leaves may be green, blue or yellow, with or without striking variegation.

Most hostas develop into rounded, dome-shaped mounds of foliage as with *Hosta sieboldiana*, but there are exceptions. A few, like *H. nigrescens* or its hybrid *H.* 'Krossa Regal', are much more upright, with the leaves carried at the tops of exceptionally long, straight leaf stalks. Others, like 'Emerald Tiara', form rather low, flattened mounds. Some, such as *H. decorata* have spreading (stoloniferous) root systems, and instead of producing individual, rounded mounds, they produce flat colonies of interlocking mounds.

The leaves of hostas consist of two parts: a stalk and a blade. The point at which the two meet is often called the 'navel'. The blade is commonly referred to as the leaf, and it is most usually heart-shaped, as in *H. sieboldiana* var. *elegans*. It can, in fact, vary from almost round (*H. tokudama*), to oval (*H. opipara*), or long and narrow (*H. longissima*). The tips of the leaves may come gradually to a long, tapering point, may come abruptly to a sharp point, or may be almost round at the tip. The base of the leaf, where it joins the leaf stalk, may be heart-shaped – with an equal lobe on either side of the leaf stalk – or it may be wedge-shaped, appearing to have been cut off straight across the bottom. The sides or margins of the leaf may gradually curve in towards the stalk, or may run into the stalk without any obvious point of separation. There are many intermediates between these forms.

The margins are always simple, in that they do not have teeth, lobes or any other form of indentation, but they can be flat as in 'Devon Green', wavy like *H. undulata* or goffered like the edge of a piecrust as in 'Donahue Piecrust'. The blade itself may vary similarly, being flat like *H. opipara*, arched like 'Jade Cascade' or cupped as in 'Love Pat'. Hosta leaves are characterized by their strongly marked pattern of veins, which appear to be impressed when seen from above and embossed when seen from below. In many hostas, these veins are deep and become a conspicuous feature, as with 'Green Acres', where the leaves appear furrowed. The actual surface finish of the leaf can be smooth like 'Camelot', puckered like seersucker, as in 'Midas Touch', almost polished like 'Invincible', or matt as in 'Sagae'. Most often, however, the leaves have a satiny finish as in 'Sum and Substance'.

It is common for hostas to exhibit juvenile and adult leaf forms, with juvenile plants having narrower leaves than those of adults. However, this is only of significance in a small number of varieties such as 'Ginko Craig', but it is often very noticeable in young plants raised in tissue culture (see p.37). Young plants of 'Halcyon' raised this way have very narrow leaves, and if you see these in a nursery you may suspect incorrect labelling, but they will mature into the typical plant with heart-shaped leaves. Hosta leaves also vary seasonally. The first leaves in spring tend to be narrower than those produced later in the season, although in one or two hostas, such as 'August Moon', the reverse is evident.

Variegation in the leaves of hostas arises as a result of damage to cells in the growing tip (or meristem) of the plant. This results in a redistribution of the pigments through the leaf. Pigments in the leaves of plants are carried in cells known as plastids. In hostas, as throughout the plant kingdom, the dominant plastids are the green ones known as chlorophyll cells. These catch the energy from sunlight and use it to manufacture the complex organic compounds that drive the

The classic Hosta fortunei *var.* albopicta *at its peak in late spring, before the variegation fades to a soft green.*

plant's metabolism. It takes only a very small variation in the atomic structure of the plastids for them to change colour, and such changes can be induced by physical damage to the cells. This may occur in the process of propagation, or it may be caused by a spade in the garden, by insect or mollusc damage, or by chemical damage. Indeed, certain chemicals and radiation are sometimes used on hostas or their seeds with the intention of damaging the meristem to induce variegation. Generally, variegated hostas are not as robust as the wild species and therefore do not survive for long in the wild, although they can be maintained in gardens by careful cultivation. Such hostas are also unstable and are liable to revert to all-green forms.

Many hostas seem to acquire their variegation gradually during summer while in others it appears to diminish, change colour or disappear altogether. The plant world has given this behaviour a variety of names depending on the nature of the metamorphosis. *H. fortunei* var. *albopicta* is an example of 'viridescence', where the leaves emerge with a pale yellow centre, which becomes progressively greener. Viridescence also applies to a leaf with white variegation that turns green. 'Gold Standard' is an example of 'lutescence', in which the leaves unfurl green and gradually become yellow or gold. 'Albescence' refers to a plant having yellow variegation that turns white, such as *H. ventricosa* 'Variegata', which has a margin that is albescent. Viridescence, lutescence and albescence are all seasonal variations, repeated again each year. If the leaves of a hosta become permanently green year after year, the hosta is said to have reverted.

Hostas with attractive foliage for flower arrangements

'Aristocrat'	'June'
'Aspen Gold'	'Lakeside Black Satin'
'Donahue Piecrust'	'Patriot'
H. fortunei var. *aureomarginata*	'Sagae'
'Frances Williams'	*H. sieboldiana* var. *elegans*
'Green Acres'	'Zounds'
'Invincible'	

A typical hosta flowerhead and fleshy scape

THE FLOWERS OF HOSTAS

The flowers of hostas are the perfect complement to their foliage. The flower stem (scape) arises directly from the roots, coming up through the leaves to carry the flowers above the foliage in a one-sided or many-sided raceme. The individual flowers are relatively large, funnel- or bell-shaped (often bell-shaped in hybrids), and flared at the mouth with usually six spreading lobes. These may be white, lavender or purple, often with more deeply toned markings. In hot climates, the flower colours may be paler than normal. The reproductive organs protrude from the flower and consist of six stamens and a single tube (stigma) which extends beyond the stamens. The stamens are upturned towards the tip like an eyelash, and the colour of the anthers is important in the identification of species.

After flowering, most hostas produce seed in chambered seed pods, which are usually the same colour as the foliage. A few hostas have purple seed pods, such as 'Cherry Berry'. The pods ripen and open about six weeks after flowering, to give shiny, oval seeds, black if fertile and pale or even white if sterile. A few varieties, mostly sterile hybrids, do not produce pods at all, and the stems wither after flowering. Fertile seed will germinate readily (see 'Growing Hostas from Seed', p.36).

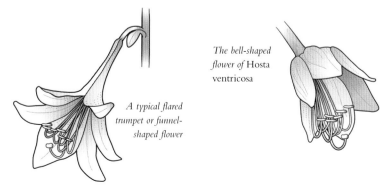

A typical flared trumpet or funnel-shaped flower

The bell-shaped flower of Hosta ventricosa

How to grow hostas

Hostas are generally regarded as shade-loving plants, tolerant of a wide variety of conditions in the garden. While this is generally true, they do require much more light than most people think. Most hostas grow well in ordinary garden soil with sun in the morning and dappled to moderate shade in the afternoon. However, to get the very best from hostas, it is important to study their individual needs more closely.

The amount of shade required by any particular hosta varies with the amount of water available to its roots. A few even prefer to grow in the sun (see 'Hostas in the Sun', p.57). The leaves of hostas often look their best when the plants are grown in dappled shade, but they flower more freely when they are grown in some sun.

Hostas are generally frost-hardy plants, and will survive winters outdoors in the following European and North American regions: in Europe, south of an imaginary line between Edinburgh in Scotland and Uppsala in Sweden, and north of an imaginary line from the southern centre of France to the north of Greece; in eastern North America, from just south of the Canadian border to the middle of Georgia and Alabama; in western North America, from Vancouver Island in Canada, south to California. These plants also flourish in similarly temperate areas throughout the world.

Winter chilling is essential to the life cycle of hostas, and if the climate is too warm, they will not survive for long. In cold climates, flowering may be aborted by early frosts. While frost will not normally damage the roots of hostas, the repeated

The huge, puckered leaves, with their seersucker surface, are the attributes that most often attract gardeners to Hosta sieboldiana *var.* elegans.

alternation of freezing and thawing can be harmful, especially to very small hostas, which may be heaved out of the ground. In most climates, hosta leaves may be damaged by late frosts.

SUPPLYING HOSTAS WITH SHADE

There is more to shade than merely keeping sun off the leaves of a plant. It actually modifies the microclimate, making the air both cooler and more humid. Shade also moderates soil moisture content, making it more evenly available to the plants through the year than would be the case if the plants were growing in the sun.

Shade can vary considerably in its density. The absence of sunlight caused by high, thin clouds is quite different in quality from the shade cast by a group of large, dense evergreen trees like yews (*Taxus*). What most hostas need is good, indirect light, but not dense shade. The ideal situation is a light, dappled shade cast by a canopy of tall trees. Good light can also be found at the foot of a north-facing wall or fence (in the Northern Hemisphere), where a plant can be out of direct sun but open to the skies above.

Using trees to provide shade

The most natural way of creating shade in a garden is to plant trees. In a small garden these are most usefully arranged in an equilateral triangle with one tree or group of trees in each corner. One side of the triangle should lie on a line running from east to west, and the third corner of the triangle should point to north (in the Northern Hemisphere). As the Earth rotates, the shade cast by these trees will move across the triangle from its western side to its eastern side. Plants at the centre of the triangle will be in shade for the whole of the day, ideal for shade tolerant hostas; those to the east or the west of the triangle will receive morning or afternoon sun respectively, which suits a great many hostas perfectly. Sun tolerant plants can be grown on the south face of the triangle.

The choice of trees is important. Certain trees, notably beeches (*Fagus*), birches (*Betula*), cherries (*Prunus*) and willows (*Salix*) root at the soil's surface and are best avoided. Their spreading roots are often visible and they compete directly for the same

The shapely leaves of Hosta 'Snowden' make a perfect foil to the diffuse lacy foliage of Geranium sylvaticum 'Album'.

moisture and nutrients as the roots of hostas, usually to their detriment. Oaks root deeply and make ideal companions for hostas, as do many genera of small ornamental trees like amelanchiers, apples (*Malus*), *Sorbus*, *Gleditsia*, *Liquidambar*, *Halesia*, *Stewartia*, *Styrax* and some magnolias, including *M. salicifolia* and *M.* × *proctoriana* and the varieties of *M.* × *loebneri*.

The problem with trees is that they keep growing. The pretty, little ornamental trees that cast just the right amount of shade when they are young, grow all too soon into trees that cast too much shade for the well-being of the hostas. Unfortunately, cutting them back all too often disfigures them. The answer may be to remove a tree from time to time.

Using artificial shade structures

Shade can be created artificially by erecting structures such as pergolas or shade houses. These structures can be covered with either roofing laths or climbing and scrambling plants. If laths are used, they should run from north to south (in the Northern Hemisphere) so that their shadow moves across the leaves of the hostas as the sun appears to cross the sky. The spacing between the laths can be varied to alter the density of their shade. It can also be useful to make the shade more dense at one end of the structure since some hostas prefer deeper shade. If roofing laths are placed their own distance apart, they will cast about 75 per cent shade but this will vary according to their thickness.

If climbing and scrambling plants are used rather than laths, similar problems arise to those created by shade-casting trees: in time, they will get too big, cast too much shade and compete with the hostas for the same moisture and nutrients. The size of some climbers, such as roses and clematis, can be controlled by regular annual pruning, although most climbers tend to increase in overall size over the years even when regularly pruned. One solution is to plant relatively closely with the aim of removing every other climber after about 10 years, or to replace them in an alternating sequence.

How much shade do hostas need?

Hostas vary considerably in the amount of shade they prefer. Most simply need light to dappled shade, such as that cast by a high tree canopy. Typically, hostas with white-margined leaves, such as 'Francee', need more shade than yellow-margined or yellow-centred hostas, like 'Twilight' and 'Paul's Glory' respectively. Green- and yellow-leaved hostas, such as 'Devon Green' and 'Aspen Gold' correspondingly, thrive in a few hours of morning sun, provided they have adequate moisture, but the majority of blue-leaved sorts, 'Halcyon' for example, lose their glaucous surface if exposed to direct sunlight. Hostas with white central variegation benefit from a little sun if they are to remain vigorous. For these, about two hours of morning sun is about right, provided that there is enough moisture at their roots; the white part of the leaves can scorch if there is too much exposure to strong sunlight and too little moisture.

The ever popular Hosta 'Gold Standard' can be difficult to site as it needs light shade but no direct sunlight.

It can sometimes be difficult to find the right amount of shade for a particular hosta, and this can only be discovered by trial and error. 'Gold Standard', for example, does not produce its striking gold and green colouring if it is in too much shade, but the leaves can scorch if it is sited in too much sun, and the difference between the one extreme and the other is quite small. In such cases, the best one can do is move the hosta around until its variegation has the depth of colour required. Where a hosta is known to have specific light requirements like this, it is mentioned under its individual entry in chapter four.

SOIL REQUIREMENTS AND PREPARATION

The perfect soil for hostas is a rich friable, slightly acid, loam with a pH of about 6. The soil should crumble in the hand when squeezed lightly. Most hostas will grow happily in any reasonably fertile, ordinary garden soil, provided that it holds moisture but is well-drained at the same time, and especially if

23

it is enriched with well-rotted organic materials, such as farmyard manure or garden compost.

Small and dwarf hostas are generally more fussy about their soil needs. They lack the vigour to establish themselves in heavy clay soils and even fairly average soils may be too much for them. They grow best in lighter, friable loam where they can develop satisfactory root systems quickly, but even then they need plenty of leafmould, well-rotted garden compost or other peat substitutes to loosen the earth to maintain an even supply of moisture at the roots.

The size and unique poise of the leaves of Hosta 'Sagae' make it an outstanding specimen plant.

Clay soils

Large and very large hostas, such as 'Sagae' and 'Frances Williams' grow very well on heavy clay soils, as do many of the medium-sized hostas with hand-sized leaves, such as 'Patriot' and *H. fortunei* var. *albopicta*. Small hostas like 'Golden Tiara' or 'Little Aurora', however, struggle against the sheer stickiness of such soils. Clay soils are usually rich in nutrients and retain moisture long after lighter soils have dried out, but their very density makes it difficult for plant roots to penetrate; many plants, including hostas, are slow to establish. The most effective way of improving heavy clay soils, and one that has stood the test of time, is to mix in coarse horticultural grit and well-rotted farmyard manure or garden compost in equal quantities by volume.

Sandy soils

All hostas, including quite small ones, grow well on sandy soils where the problems they face are quite different. Their roots penetrate the soil easily and they quickly make surprisingly large and complex root systems. The problem with such soils is that they drain quickly. Water falling on sandy soils is not retained; it passes straight through, leaching out nutrients.

The best way to improve the long-term fertility of sandy soil is to add copious quantities of organic materials, preferably in the form of well-rotted farmyard or stable manure, or garden compost. As these materials decompose, they act as a sponge in the soil, retaining moisture and nutrients. It may also be useful to add these materials annually as a mulch around the plants every autumn. Sandy soils tend to be low in nutrients, so they also need feeding. Concentrated organic fertilizers, such as chicken manure pellets and proprietary concentrated animal manure, forked lightly into the surface of the soil in late winter will increase the levels of nitrogen and other nutrients in the soil.

Chalky soils

Although hostas are generally easy-going about their soil requirements, they are not happy on thin soils over chalk. The alkalinity of such soils causes the green in hosta leaves to turn a sickly, chlorotic yellow, and blue hosta leaves to become blotched with dull green. Such soils are often extremely sharp-draining, which compounds the problems, and hostas grown in them tend to look thin and weedy because there is insufficient moisture at their roots. There is no real solution to this problem other than to grow hostas in raised beds filled with imported, non-chalky soil.

SHELTERING HOSTAS

Shelter from harsh, buffeting winds is as essential to hostas as shade and adequate moisture at their roots. Strong winds not only physically damage the large leaves of hostas by bruising, splitting and tearing them, but also causes scorching through dessication; wind moving across the leaves of hostas dries them, just as it dries laundry on a line. Problems arise when the amount of moisture being drawn out of the leaves by wind is greater than the amount of moisture that can be supplied by the roots. The leaves then wither leaving brown, desiccated patches. The problem is not solved by adding more water to the soil, but by reducing the flow of the wind.

Hedges, trees and shrubs break or filter the force of the wind, and slow it down. Inflexible structures such as buildings, walls and fences, however, may actually accelerate the wind by causing downdraughts, eddies and other damaging air currents, particularly in interior corners of buildings. Hostas that are being damaged by such air currents should be moved to a more sheltered position.

The best way to shelter hostas from damaging winds is to plant them out of the direct path of the prevailing wind or to partly surround them by shrubs or trees. On exposed sites and in new gardens, it may be advisable to put up a low, temporary plastic windbreak. This may be unsightly, but it will prove invaluable in the short term.

PLANTING HOSTAS IN THE OPEN GARDEN

How well a hosta does in the garden depends almost entirely upon the amount of trouble taken to prepare the ground before planting (see also 'Soil Requirements and Preparation', p.23). No amount of feeding or watering after the event will ever make up for poor preparation of the ground at planting time.

Hostas are best planted either in spring, while the soil is warming up, or else in late summer or early autumn when it is still warm from summer. Warmth in the soil enables their roots to establish quickly. Planting time is not critical, however, and established clumps can be moved at almost any time of year, provided that all the leaves are cut off if they are moved during the growing season. More important is that the soil is properly prepared, preferably well in advance, and that after planting, the hostas should be watered in well and not allowed to dry out in the weeks that follow. Moving hostas when they are in leaf helps to get their spacing right because their size and shape is evident.

If an individual hosta is to be planted, the size of the planting hole is determined by the ultimate size to which the hosta is expected to grow. Very large hostas, such as 'Sagae', 'Blue Angel' and 'Jade Cascade', can make a mound of foliage as much as 1.2m (4ft) across after five years, and so they need a planting hole as large as for a shrub – about 1m (3ft) across and about 45cm (18in) deep. Smaller hostas need proportionately smaller planting holes; a hole 45cm (18in) across and 30cm (12in) deep is sufficient for a small hosta like 'Golden Tiara'. For very small or dwarf hostas, the provision of a suitable growing medium is more important than the size of the hole.

The small, heart-shaped leaves of Hosta 'Golden Tiara' make dense, symmetrical mounds in pots but its habit is more diffuse in a border.

Firstly, the soil should be removed from the hole and set to one side and the soil at the bottom of the hole broken up with a fork. The hole should then be filled with alternating layers of well-rotted farmyard or stable manure (or garden compost) and the original soil. Each layer should be well trodden down before the next layer is added. If the soil is heavy, coarse sand or grit should be added to the manure. Ideally, planting holes should be prepared several weeks before planting, which allows the soil to settle.

If one is planting a whole bed of hostas, or if they are to be planted in drifts, then the whole area needs to be prepared, rather than individual holes. Several months before planting, the whole area should be dug over to the depth of two spade blades, incorporating organic manure or garden compost,

The solid leaves of Hosta 'Green Gold' and the simplicity of its grey-blue pot make a striking contrast with the lacy white-painted iron railings and daisy.

taking care not to mix the fertile topsoil with the less fertile subsoil. It should then be top-dressed with a mulch of well-rotted organic material. Individual planting holes can then be dug as and when needed.

Hostas should be planted so their crowns (the place where the leaves and roots meet) are level with the finished soil level, or at the same level as the potting compost in the pot. New hostas purchased from nurseries or garden centres are mostly supplied in pots, and they often have very congested roots. On planting, tease out these congested roots and spread them out into the planting hole. Some of the potting compost in which the plant was growing may be lost, and some of the roots may break off, but this is not important; it will simply encourage plants to put on new, vigorous roots.

Once in the planting hole, the soil should be returned around the hosta and then firmed with your heel. Finally, soak the soil around the hosta, which is best achieved by leaving a hose trickling slowly into the soil around the hosta rather than by swamping it with a deluge of water from a can. Take care not to drown the hosta by leaving the hose running too long or too fast. Afterwards, mulch the soil around the plant with plenty of well-rotted organic material to conserve moisture.

PLANTING HOSTAS IN CONTAINERS

As a rule, hostas in containers are best grown in a soil-based potting medium, especially if the containers are large. Experience shows that peat-based potting mixes are difficult to manage in large containers, since the compost tends to dry out and is then difficult to re-wet, while frequent watering means that nutrients are quickly leached out. The first choice for containers, therefore, should be a proprietary soil-based potting compost, such as John Innes No. 3. Very small hostas, however, such as *H. venusta* and 'Masquerade', seem to do best in peat-based potting composts to which some extra horticultural grit has been added. All hostas in containers will need regular feeding and watering (see pp.31–33).

The containers should always have adequate drainage holes at the bottom, and these holes should be covered with a thick

layer of drainage materials such as crocks from broken pots or old roofing tiles, taking care not to block the drainage holes. Some people like to cover the drainage materials with a layer of well-rotted farmyard or stable manure, but the problem with doing this is that the manure will shrink and the plant will finish up lower down in the pot than was intended. Hostas in pots should be planted using the same basic method as for planting in the open garden (see p.26), using potting compost instead of garden soil. Once planted, hostas in containers also need to be watered in thoroughly.

Even when well fed and watered, hostas in containers eventually exhaust the growing medium and need to be re-potted. As a rule, this should be done every three or four years. The hosta should be taken out of its container and the growing medium shaken off its roots. The container and the crocks should then be thoroughly washed with a mild disinfectant, before the hosta is replanted using fresh potting compost. If necessary, the hosta can be moved on to a new or larger pot.

Hosta undulata var. undulata is one of the most unstable of variegated hostas, as can be seen from the varying widths of the central white stripe.

The spacing of hostas

When planting hostas, it is often difficult to know how far apart to set them from each other or from other plants. Much depends on how long they are expected to remain in the same place, on the ultimate effect that is desired, and on the size of the hosta to be planted.

Most hostas form graceful mounds of leaves and therefore look best if planted with sufficient space around them to reveal their shape and form. Several hostas, however, such as *H. lancifolia*, *H. tardiflora* and *H. undulata* var. *undulata*, are displayed to best effect when planted in long strings or rows at the front edge of a border, or along the side of a path. In such cases, the young plants should be set out side by side and quite close together.

Most books about hostas and most plant labels give the expected ultimate spread and height of individual plants. To achieve a planting with sufficient space around the hostas, plant them so that the centre of the hosta is the same distance as its expected spread from the edges of the plants nearest to it. Hostas look particularly good when planted in drifts because of the way their leaves overlap. To create a drift, space the plants so that their centres are half the sum of their expected spreads apart. The growth of hostas varies greatly on different soils and between different gardens, and ultimately the only way to judge the planting distances correctly is from experience.

Watering hostas

Hostas will only have healthy, turgid leaves if they receive adequate moisture at their roots. It is this moisture that gives the leaves their sheen and accentuates their puckering and width of variegation. By day, a hosta absorbs water through its roots and gives off water vapour through its leaves, creating a partial vacuum that causes the roots to draw in more water from the soil. This internal pressure keeps the leaves of hostas plumped up and fleshy. If the supply of water is restricted, however, a moisture deficit occurs throughout the plant, causing the leaves to become smaller and misshapen.

Hostas need a constant supply of moisture deep in the soil. This is best supplied by applying water directly to the roots of the hosta, beneath the leaves, using either a watering can without its rose or a hosepipe left trickling under the leaf mound for several hours at a time. Seep hoses, which appear to sweat when turned on, can also be threaded around clumps and left to apply water for one or two days at a time. Aim to maintain soil moisture at a reasonably constant level, watering as early in the morning as possible so that the hostas can gain maximum benefit. Avoid watering in the evening if possible, since the moisture tends to attract slugs and snails.

Hostas do not benefit from a quick sprinkle over the top every day, and the only time overhead watering can be beneficial is when it contains a foliar feed. A spray of water not only disfigures the surface of the leaves, but is also not adequate to soak into the ground to any depth. As a result, the roots grow upwards to try to get what little moisture is available at the surface, and the plant fails to develop deep, life-sustaining roots. Such shallow-rooted hostas become even more vulnerable to drought.

The same basic principles apply to hostas in containers. Most will need to be watered every two to three days from the time the leaves start to emerge in spring until they die down in autumn. Large hostas may need to be watered every day in high summer, using at least 4.5 litres (1 gallon) of water per plant. Mature specimens of large and very large hostas, especially those growing in full sun, will need a phenomenal amount of water, as much as 12 litres (3 gallons), every day. Water-retaining granules can be mixed into the potting compost on planting, but as far as hostas are concerned, they are in no way a substitute for proper watering. Furthermore, if the hostas are watered properly and are in a suitable medium, there is a danger these granules could keep them too wet.

FEEDING HOSTAS

Hostas only attain their maximum size, true colouring and character if there is sufficient nourishment available to their roots. This is particularly true of the larger sorts. In order to produce their luxuriant leaves, hostas make enormous demands on the available nutrients, especially nitrogen, and these need to be replenished regularly. It is also important to appreciate that while mulches of organic materials may add nitrogen to the soil in the long term, they can actually create a nitrogen deficit in the short term. For this reason, always add a nitrogen-rich fertilizer to any organic mulch. An excess of nitrogen, however, will produce soft and sappy growth, which is singularly attractive to slugs and snails. Potash (or potassium) in the fertilizer helps leaves to toughen up by building firm cell walls, and phosphorus in the fertilizer is important for healthy root growth.

The various elements in fertilizers are expressed as N for nitrogen, P for potassium and K for phosphorus. About once a fortnight, from late spring to midsummer, apply a weak solution of balanced fertilizer with all three elements present in equal quantities and some trace elements, which are also essential for plant health. Only one application of a high-nitrogen fertilizer, which contains twice as much nitrogen as potassium, is necessary in early spring. Remember to feed hostas in containers in the same way; potting composts usually only contain sufficient nutrients to keep the plants fed for a few weeks, so after that the plants will depend entirely on additional feeding.

Fertilizers can be obtained in various forms, in powders, pellets, granules or liquids. These can be applied directly to the soil or they can be mixed in water and applied through a hosepipe or watering can to the soil or to the foliage. Bulky organic manures also contain many of these elements; but the quantities and proportions are uncertain. They do, however, have the added benefit of improving the texture and quality of the soil in ways that inorganic fertilizers cannot.

Fertilizers should be applied to hostas any time from spring until midsummer; later applications promote soft, sappy growth, which is prone to pest and disease damage. Fertilizers and manures should be applied around the hostas in doughnut-like rings, so that they do not cover the crown of the hosta. Only foliar feeds should be applied over the crown of the hostas, preferably when they are in leaf. Liquid feeds intended for soil application could also be applied over the crown, but only while the plant is dormant; if it is in leaf, the feed will discolour the leaves.

MULCHING HOSTAS

Mulches are organic materials applied to the surface of the soil, and their chief function is to reduce the rate of evaporation of moisture from the soil surface. They may also contain a certain amount of nutrients, and as they rot down and become incorporated into the soil, they greatly improve it. Mulches may be of shredded bark, which will contribute little or nothing in the way of plant nutrients, or they may be of bulky materials like farmyard or stable manure, mushroom and garden compost, all of which contribute small amounts of plant foods, as well as reducing evaporation and improving soil structure.

Mulches should be applied to the soil around, but not touching the crowns of, hostas in autumn or early winter, so that the winter rains can wash any nutrients through them and into the soil. When they are spread, do not allow the mulch to touch the crowns of hostas, as the mulch may suppress and distort the soft, new leaves as they emerge.

Mulching not only improves the appearance of this bed of newly planted hostas, but also helps to retain moisture in the soil. Hosta 'Borwick Beauty' dominates this planting in dappled shade.

Bark mulches can be applied at any time of year. Mulch needs to be renewed annually, although it is not necessary to always use the same materials. In fact, it may be beneficial to vary the mulching materials to ensure that a wider spectrum of plant nutrients reaches the roots of the hostas.

PROPAGATING HOSTAS

Hostas can be increased either by seed or by division, but the only way to be sure that a new hosta will look like the one you started with is to divide it.

Division

The simplest way to divide an established hosta clump is to take a slice out of it, rather like taking a slice out of a circular cake. The slice can be as large as a quarter of the entire clump, in which case it can be further divided into smaller pieces. Simply cut through the slice with a sharp knife, which has been dipped in fungicide beforehand. The cut surfaces of the new small pieces should then be dusted with a fungicide after the cut is made, and then potted up or planted out to grow. Fill the hole left in the original clump with sifted soil, and after one or two years it will look as though the original hosta had never been disturbed.

Two other methods of division include: lifting the whole clump out of the ground and splitting it in half, using two garden forks back-to-back as levers, or teasing apart every single fan of leaves or buds with roots attached by hand or with the aid of a knife. The root systems of hostas vary greatly. *H. sieboldiana*, for example, forms tough and very dense, almost woody crowns, which can be hard to divide. Others, such as *H. sieboldii*, have diffuse and rather loose root systems, which can be shaken or pulled apart with ease. Most hostas lie in between these two extremes.

Hostas are best divided in early spring just as the new season's shoots are appearing above ground, but early autumn is often preferred in warmer regions as the ground is still warm enough for the plants to establish new roots before winter. They can be divided in summer when in full growth, provided that the leaves are cut down first and they are given plenty of water after replanting. However, it is possible to divide hostas at almost any time of the year, apart from times of frost or prolonged drought.

Growing hostas from seed

Hostas can be grown from seed almost too easily, and unless the seedheads are removed after flowering, some varieties will seed themselves quite freely on some soils. Most self-sown hosta seedlings have little garden value and they bear only a passing resemblance to their parents. *H. ventricosa* is the only hosta whose seedlings come true, owing to some peculiarities of its reproductive system. The only way to obtain worthwhile seedlings from hostas is to pursue a deliberate breeding programme with a specific objective in mind (see 'Breeding and Hybridizing Hostas', p.37).

Hosta seeds germinate very readily, whether sown fresh or after winter storage. If seed is to be stored, take care over its collection and winnowing. Ideally, the pods should be picked as soon as they start to open and placed in a paper envelope where they can be left to open fully, shedding their seeds inside the envelope. Never use a plastic bag. Once dry, tip the contents of the envelope onto a sheet of white paper, and carefully separate the seeds from the husks and any other debris. This is an important step as the debris may contain diseases that might stop the seeds germinating or cause death after germination. Finally, put the seeds into a fresh paper envelope and place it inside a small tin. Store the tin in a refrigerator until spring. Good seeds should remain viable for six months.

The seeds of hostas are shed about six weeks after flowering.

Hosta seeds are frost hardy and can be sown indoors or out. Either way, take precautions against slugs and snails (see 'Pests and Diseases', p.39). Outdoors, seed can be sown straight into beds where it is to germinate, or in containers. Wrap containers in close-mesh chicken wire to prevent vermin eating the seeds; this seems to be less of a problem when seeds are sown in beds. The seeds can also be sown in containers or trays indoors, in a greenhouse or in a cold frame. Once the seeds have germinated in their containers, the seedlings should be kept watered and shaded until they are big enough to prick out into single pots or to line out in rows in the garden.

Micropropagation (tissue culture)

This is a form of division where whole plants are grown from single cells. It is a laboratory technique that requires a microscope and totally sterile conditions. The single cells are started into growth in test tubes in nutrient-rich jelly, and then they are grown on as plugs in trays of up to 100 plants and potted on into 8–13cm (3–5in) containers before being sold to retailers. Some hostas can take several seasons to assume their true character, while others are instantly recognizable. In the main, however, the leaf blades are narrower for up to three years when increased by this method.

BREEDING AND HYBRIDIZING HOSTAS

The purpose of breeding hostas is to raise plants that appear, at least in the eye of the breeder, to be an improvement on other hostas. Anyone trying to breed hostas should be clear as to the type of improvement they are seeking, be it thicker leaves or larger flowers. The starting point is to select parents likely to produce the desired offspring and to have a passing knowledge of the Mendelian laws of inheritance.

The reproductive organs of a hosta consist of six stamens (the male organs) and carpels (the female organs) made up of a stigma, style and ovary. At the tip of each stamen is an anther, which produces pollen. Flowers are pollinated when pollen is placed on the tip of the stigma, and this leads to fertilization of ovules within the ovary. Seeds then develop and ripen about six weeks later.

Hybridization can be performed by taking pollen from a selected parent (called the pollen parent) and deliberately placing it on the stigma of the female parent (the pod parent). Much of the skill in hybridizing consists of preventing the pod parent from being pollinated by accident through the activity of bees or other insects. The normal practice is to emasculate the pod parent before the flower opens naturally. Just as the selected flower is on the point of opening, slit open the bud using a razor blade to expose the reproductive organs, and cut away the petals and sepals. Finally, remove the anthers to prevent self-pollination. Bees and other insects now have no platform on which to land and cannot pollinate what is left.

Transfer pollen from the anther of the pollen parent to the stigma of the pod parent by brushing the anther (using the filament as a handle) across the tip of the stigma. It is crucially important that the pollen is ripe and the stigma receptive. Ripe pollen has a powder-like texture, and the stigma is receptive when it becomes sticky and swollen; once moisture appears at its tip, like a drop of dew, the moment has passed. The most successful matings take place about mid-morning, and the best chances of success are when the same flower is pollinated two or three times during the same day. Some breeders prefer to transfer the pollen using a small, camel-hair paintbrush, but it can be difficult to clean the pollen from the brush before attempting the next cross. Methylated spirits seems to be an effective cleaning agent, but allow the brush to dry afterwards.

It is important to label each cross by tying a small label to the stalk of the flower that has been pollinated. Each label should bear the date of the cross and the name of both the pollen and the pod parents. The same information should also be recorded in a record book and should follow the seed and seedlings until maturity. Seeds should be collected and sown as described on p.36.

It takes three to four years before the seedlings can be evaluated. At this stage, worthless seedlings, should be discarded or you will soon be swamped by worthless plants. Most often, worthless seedlings do not improve as they mature. Even the most successful breeders usually find that less than five per cent of their seedlings are worth growing to maturity. If breeding for improved flowers, a higher proportion of seedlings should be kept and grown on, since the first season's flowers may not be typical. Plants grown for foliage should be mature enough to produce 15 or more leaves before their penultimate assessment. It can take up to seven years for a hosta to produce its adult leaves.

If you succeed in producing a worthwhile hosta, you may want to name and register it with the International Registration Authority for Hostas, who can be contacted through the British Hosta and Hemerocallis Society (see 'Further Information', p.93). In this context, a worthwhile hosta is one that is definitely distinct from all other hostas, is uniform and stable in its characteristics, and maintains these characteristics when propagated.

PESTS AND DISEASES

Well-nourished, well-grown hostas are far less likely to be damaged by pests and diseases than those that are neglected. Hostas are generally healthy, robust plants seldom troubled by disease, but in some gardens there are two pests that are inseparable from the growing of hostas: slugs and snails.

Slugs and snails

A vast variety of remedies are offered through garden centres and magazines and these vary considerably in their efficacy. The regimen I find most successful is to apply a liquid metaldehyde formulation in late winter before the hostas emerge. In the Northern Hemisphere, the starting date of St. Valentine's day – 14th February – is easy to remember. Applications should be made every two weeks thereafter until the hostas have unfurled their leaves. The advantage of starting so early is that the metaldehyde kills the tiny black keeled slugs that lurk under the surface of the soil.

Once the leaves have emerged, pellets containing metaldehyde may be used sparingly, and their use should be continued until the leaves die down in the autumn; be especially vigilant in mid- to late summer, which is the breeding season for slugs. The pellets contain a chemical

Slugs and snails can reduce many hosta leaves to tatters unless preventative measures are taken.

attractant, however, and their excessive use simply attracts more slugs and snails into the garden. With any product designed to destroy slugs and snails, it is important to read and follow the maker's instructions. Most of the pellets available in the UK are deliberately coloured blue, which birds find difficult to see (birds actually see blue as brown).

For gardeners concerned about the possible poisoning of birds and pets, a number of products are available that claim to be safer. Many of these are based on aluminium sulphate, which is reasonably effective, but it needs to be applied more frequently than metaldehyde pellets.

Other products also aim to prevent slugs and snails from reaching plants. One product is available in toothpaste-like tubes or as tapes. Slugs are said to avoid copper strips placed around plants, but these products are expensive if needed in large quantities. Slugs and snails can be collected by hand, especially on warm, damp evenings when they are easy to find.

An alternative approach is biological control, using a nematode that parasitizes slugs. It is a highly effective way of controlling them, but it is specific to slugs and does no harm to snails, which may multiply to fill the niche vacated by the slugs. The nematode is supplied in a sachet, the contents of which are mixed with water in a can and then applied to the areas where slugs are to be eliminated. The nematodes are only effective at times when the soil is moist and above 5°C (41°F), and they should be applied directly to soil rather than to a mulch, since the slugs live in the soil not in the mulch lying over it.

The natural role of slugs and snails is to clean up the dead and decaying vegetation in gardens, and a measure of control can be obtained by removing all fallen leaves and keeping the garden free of rotting wood or anything that provides a congenial winter hiding place. Mulches provide an ideal winter hideaway for slugs and snails, so they should be disturbed from time to time and any lurking slugs and snails removed.

Slugs and snails are just as likely to eat hosta leaves when they are above the ground in containers as they are in garden borders. If hostas are grown as specimen plants near the house, every hole or lacy leaf will be an eyesore. To deter slugs and snails from climbing into containers, raise the containers above the ground on wooden blocks or terracotta feet designed for the purpose, then smear a continuous band of Vaseline around the widest part of the container. Frequently remove all debris from under and around the containers, leaving nowhere for the molluscs to hide.

Vine weevils

The presence of vine weevils is manifested by a series of distinctive notches in the edges of hosta leaves. Plump, cream-coloured grubs up to 1cm (½in) long with brown heads do their damage by eating the plant's roots, which can kill large, well-established specimens. Vine weevils have become a more frequent problem since certain chemicals were banned, especially with container-grown plants in peat-based potting composts. The simplest remedy if growing in pots is to use

A garden slug about to feast on the tender new foliage of Hosta 'Aristocrat'.

a soil-based potting compost or, if you prefer to use a soil-less potting compost, to ensure that they are repotted into fresh growing compost every year. There are now potting composts available that contain an insecticide, imidacloprid, which gives protection for up to a year. Vine weevils are also problem in damp places like bog gardens. There is a nematode biological control that can be used to control them, but this needs to be used in late summer before the grubs are large enough to cause severe damage and while the soil temperature is in the range of 12–20°C (54–68°F).

The distinctive notch made by an adult vine weevil.

Pest-resistant hostas

'Aspen Gold'	'June'
'Blue Dimples'	'Krossa Regal'
'Blue Moon'	'Leather Sheen'
'Blue Umbrellas'	*H. sieboldiana* and forms
'Camelot'	'Silvery Slugproof'
'Invincible'	'Sum and Substance'

Necrotic spots

Tiny brown spots with a central pinhole sometimes appear on the leaves in late spring if the weather has been unusually cold and damp. Fungi like grey mould (*Botrytis cinerea*) can then infect the leaves. Warmer weather and good air circulation will prevent its return, and subsequent growth will come through normally.

Viral infections

Plants are more liable to suffer from viral infections if grown in large collections without a variety of plants from other genera. Hostas are not immune to this problem, and there are several different viruses to which they can be susceptible. Signs of viral infection can be yellow mottling of the leaves, usually on just part of the leaf, rather than all of it. This mottling usually fades by midsummer. Another type of virus causes hosta leaves to become distorted, although this symptom is sometimes mistaken for drought damage. Nowadays, the advice is to burn infected plants before they can spread the virus to other hostas. There is no known cure.

Melting out

The term melting out is applied to a kind of physiological damage that occurs to the leaves of some hostas, mainly those with a white, central variegation. A brown mark appears at the centre of the leaf, which gradually dries up and falls away, leaving a hole. This damage usually occurs on tender young leaves exposed to intense sunlight, but in a few hostas it even occurs in quite dense shade.

Other problems

Although rampant in the United States, foliar nematodes or eelworms are not yet a real problem in the UK or the rest of Europe. Crown rot only occurs in hot, humid conditions, and heaving of the soil during periods of freeze/thaw conditions, which exposes the hosta roots, occurs in severe winters. Hostas are also susceptible to damage by deer, rabbits and voles; most general gardening books give advice about these pests.

HOSTAS IN THE GARDEN

CREATING SHADE AND SHELTER FOR HOSTAS

In gardens, hostas are most often grown in naturalistic settings sheltered from direct sun by large trees, but considerable thought needs to be given to the sorts of trees used, as some are much more suitable than others (See 'Using Trees to Provide Shade', pp.20–21).

Smaller decorative trees are more useful for gardens with limited space or where shade needs to be created quickly. Ideal small trees include the crab apples (*Malus*). Many of these have pretty, colourful blossom in spring and showy fruits in autumn, although several of the most ornamental crab apples tend to make low crowns, which can be a problem when planting beneath them. *Malus hupehensis* has an upright and narrow, vase-shaped outline, which makes it an ideal tree, especially useful for small gardens. Other very decorative trees that cast the right sort of light shade include the service tree (*Amelanchier lamarckii*), the mountain ash or rowan (*Sorbus aucuparia*), the whitebeam (*Sorbus aria*), the honey locust (*Gleditsia triacanthos*) and *Liquidambar styraciflua*. Some of the smaller magnolias are also suitable, including *Magnolia salicifolia*, *M. × proctoriana*, and *M. × loebneri* cultivars like the pink-flowered 'Leonard Messel' and the fragrant, white-flowered 'Merrill', as are several of the arborescent dogwoods, such as *Cornus nuttallii* and *C. kousa*. Other suitable subjects are listed in the 'Shade Providers' box on p.47.

Shrubby plants can also be used to cast shade around hostas, even though their more important role is to slow the flow of

Hosta hypoleuca, whose native habitat is hot, sunny mountainsides, produces lusher foliage when grown in the garden.

wind through the garden. Especially useful are those that arise from a single stem at ground level and those that arise out of the ground vertically and then arch outwards. Among the most suitable are the witch hazels (*Hamamelis*) – especially the forms of *H. × intermedia, H. mollis, H. japonica* and the small-flowered *H. vernalis* – and several viburnums, including the tall, winter-flowering *Viburnum × bodnantense* and its cultivars 'Dawn', 'Deben' and 'Charles Lamont', and the fragrant *V. farreri*.

The more tree-like forms of *Cotoneaster* are highly suitable, including *C. fridgida* 'Cornubia' and the yellow-fruiting 'Rothschildianus', as are most of the hazels (*Corylus*), especially *C. avellana* and its cultivars 'Aurea' and 'Contorta', and *C. maxima* 'Purpurea'; the shrubby, multi-stemmed, summer-flowering magnolias with fragrant flowers are also appropriate, such as *Magnolia wilsonii, M. sieboldii* subsp. *sinensis, M. × wieseneri* and *M. × thompsoniana. Photinia × fraseri* 'Birmingham' and

A sumptuous planting of varied hostas flourishing in a woodland setting.

'Red Robin' both make small, shrubby trees and are interesting on account of the red colouring of their new leaves. *Osmanthus heterophyllus* in its several forms is a useful evergreen, producing fragrant flowers in autumn.

On acid soils, *Disanthus cercidifolius* contributes the most amazing autumn colour, and hydrangeas look wonderful underplanted with perennials like the late-flowering *Hosta tardiflora*, dwarf asters and liriopes in shades of mauve-blue and purple, although all these plants will grow in any fertile soil. A number of elegant, shade-loving shrubs are grown with hostas on acid soils, and among the loveliest of these are the daintier rhododendrons, such as *Rhododendron augustinii* and *R. yunnanense*, and azaleas (large types with dense foliage are unsuitable), *Zenobia pulverulenta*, camellias and pieris, especially the taller ones like *Pieris formosa* and its many cultivars. These shade-loving shrubs do not need an overhead canopy of their own if they are growing at the foot of a shady wall or fence.

Some shrubs are unsuitable for casting shade on hostas because they form dense mats of fibrous roots. Chief among these are box (*Buxus*) and hollies (*Ilex*). Lilacs (*Syringa*) and ornamental privets (*Ligustrum*) are also unsuitable because their greedy roots dry out and exhaust the surrounding soil.

In the wild, some hostas grow in damp meadows where their leaves are shaded by the leaves of eulalia grasses (*Miscanthus sinensis*) or by clump-forming bamboos. In the garden, suitable shade-casting bamboos might include *Fargesia murieliae*, *F. nitida* and *F. robusta*, the tiny-leaved *Thamnocalamus crassinodus*, or the Chilean or foxtail bamboo (*Chusquea culeou*).

Shade providers

Large trees

Carya (Hickories)	*Podocarpus*
Larix (Larches)	*Populus* (Poplars)
Picea (Spruces)	*Quercus* (Oaks)
Pinus (Pines)	

Small decorative trees

Acer palmatum cultivars
  (Japanese maples)
Amelanchier lamarckii
  (Service tree)
Cercidiphyllum japonicum
  (Kadsura tree)
Cornus (Taller dogwoods)
Gleditsia triacanthos (Honey
  locust)
Halesia monticola var. *vestita*
  (Silver bell tree)
Liquidambar styraciflua

Magnolia (Smaller
  magnolias)
Malus (Crab apples)
Nyssa sylvatica (Black
  tupelo)
Sophora japonica (Japanese
  pagoda tree)
Sorbus aria (Whitebeam)
Sorbus aucuparia (Mountain
  ash or rowan)
Stewartia monodelpha
Stewartia pseudocamellia

Shrubs

Camellias
Corylus (Hazel)
Cotoneasters (tree-like
  cultivars)
Disanthus cercidifolius
Hamamelis (Witch hazel)
Hydrangeas
Magnolias (shrubby
  cultivars)
Osmanthus heterophyllus
  and cultivars

Photinia × *fraseri*
  'Birmingham' and 'Red
  Robin'
Pieris (taller cultivars)
Rhododendrons and
  azaleas (smaller cultivars)
Viburnums
Zenobia pulverulenta

Grasses and bamboos

Chusquea culeou (Chilean
  or foxtail bamboo)
Fargesia murielae
Fargesia nitida
Fargesia robusta

Miscanthus sinensis
  (Eulalia grasses)
Thamnocalamus crassinodus

COMPANIONS FOR HOSTAS IN SHADE

Hostas are grown primarily for their foliage, so they associate well with other plants that have very visual foliage, and ferns are the obvious choice.

Hostas with ferns

Dynamic displays can be made by growing hostas with ferns, the majority of which have very finely cut leaves, and with the linear-leaved sedges (*Carex*). All grow happily in the same conditions as hostas, but the ferns should be sited where the shade is deepest. For example, *Hosta* 'Francee' can be combined with the fern *Polystichum setiferum* Divisilobum Group and the sedge *Carex conica* 'Snowline', which has narrow leaves with thin white margins. In this grouping, the wintergreen quality of the fern and the sedge carry interest through the winter when the hosta is dormant. Several ferns have dark green, glossy fronds that last all through winter, and among the best of these are the Christmas fern (*Polysticum acrostichoides)* and the western sword fern (*P. munitum*). Further interest can be created by underplanting the hosta with snowdrops.

Other ferns that look particularly good with hostas include the dainty Lady fern (*Athyrium filix-femina*), the more robust male fern (*Dryopteris filix-mas*), the common British polypod (*Polypodium vulgare*) and the southern polypod (*P. cambricum*); many highly decorative forms exist of all of these. The Japanese painted fern (*Athyrium niponicum* var. *pictum*) has silvery grey fronds with claret-stained centres. *Athyrium otophorum* var. *okonum*

The filigree fronds of Adiantum pedatum and an acanthus accentuate the outline and texture of the enormous hosta leaves.

has fronds of similar colouring but these form upright shuttlecocks; both ferns look wonderful with blue-leaved hostas and heucheras like *Heuchera* 'Amethyst Myst', 'Blackbird' and 'Chocolate Ruffles'.

Very large-growing ferns like *Osmunda regalis, Woodwardia fimbriata* and Goldie's fern *(Dryopteris goldieana)* are really only suitable for use with the largest of hostas, such as *Hosta* 'Krossa Regal' and 'Jade Cascade', and even then, the ferns are best used as a background. Ferns that run at the roots, such as the sensitive fern (*Onoclea sensibilis*), the shuttlecock fern (*Matteuccia struthiopteris*) and the king fern (*M. pennsylvanica*), form large colonies and may, in time, suffocate any hostas in their way, even large, vigorous hostas.

Shade-tolerant perennials with hostas

Almost any shade-tolerant perennial will grow with hostas. Some seem to create the perfect partnership either in leaf or flower, whereas others like Lenten roses (*Helleborus orientalis*) are merely useful because they flower early in the year, before hostas come into leaf. Dicentras, most notably *Dicentra formosa*, with its finely cut grey leaves and dangling lockets of pink or white flowers, make fine companions to hostas early in the season, although some varieties will swamp smaller hostas unless care is taken to control them. *Dicentra* 'Bacchanal', with its dark glaucous green leaves and claret-coloured lockets, makes a charming picture planted in front of *Hosta* 'Northern Exposure'.

The spreading, pale-green-leaved *Corydalis ochroleuca* is more delicate than the dicentras, but it could cope with the competition of *Hosta* 'Jade Cascade' or the smaller-leaved 'Devon Green'. The heucheras with greener leaves, such as *Heuchera* 'Eco Magnififolia' or the newer 'Ring of Fire', will also look good with *Hosta* 'Devon Green'. Hardy geraniums with lavender-blue flowers are picked up by the soft glaucous blue tones of *Hosta* 'Love Pat' and 'Blue Moon'. If blue-flowered *Brunnera macrophylla* 'Langtrees' and *Omphalodes cappadocica* 'Starry Eyes' were added, a symphony of blue shades could be created, maybe sharpened up by *Hosta* 'Zounds' with its brassy yellow foliage.

Many hostas, such as Hosta 'Blue Angel', will thrive in moist conditions.

Hostas in open woodland

A number of plants associated with woodlands make ideal companions for hostas. Solomon's seal (*Polygonatum*), especially the taller forms like *P. × hybridum*, makes a complete contrast in form; their tall, elegant stems with two ranks of leaves, and their pendant white flowers are totally different from the rounded mounds of hosta leaves and their spire-like flower spikes. The low-growing *Disporopsis pernyi*, which is in effect an evergreen, broad-leaved Solomon's seal, is useful for its winter presence. The closely related *Smilacina racemosa* is similar in growth to Solomon's seal, emerging from asparagus-like shoots and producing fluffy white flowers in mid-spring.

A beautifully composed picture of colour opposites and foliage contrasts: the blue-leaved Hosta 'Halcyon', the yellow-leaved grass Hakonechloa macra *'Aureola' with the subtler lime-green of* Euphorbia amygdaloides.

One of its great merits is that the foliage remains green well into autumn. *Smilacina stellata* is similar but is seen in gardens less often.

Several saxifrages are excellent woodland and shade plants, and the finest of these is *Saxifraga fortunei*, lovely both in leaf and in flower. The somewhat begonia-like leaves are roundish and scalloped, shiny green above and paler below, and they are carried on long stalks, which are often reddish towards the ground. Garden varieties tend to have varying degrees of reddish brown hues in the leaves and leaf stalks, and this is especially marked in 'Rubrifolia'. This saxifrage makes an excellent foil to hostas, since red is not found in the leaves of hostas. The white flowers of *S. fortunei* are produced in October (in southern England) on slender stems well above the leaves and are composed of long and narrow, mostly drooping petals. These flowers marry well with those of *Hosta tardiflora*, which produces its spikes of lavender flowers at the same time and is the last hosta to flower. Some more recently introduced varieties of *Saxifraga fortunei* have almost black leaves and red flowers; one of the best of these is 'Black Ruby'.

Another way to introduce red foliage into a hosta border is to use the red-leaved plantain (*Plantago major* 'Rubrifolia'), which people sometimes mistake for a hosta because of the similarity of the leaf shapes. This is an understandable mistake as hostas are sometimes called plantain lilies because of this similarity.

Hostas with ornamental grasses

The contrasting leaf shapes of ornamental grasses and hostas create an immediate visual impact. While the leaves of hostas are usually broad and heart-shaped, those of grasses are essentially linear. Golden Hakone grass (*Hakonechloa macra* 'Alboaurea'), or the very similar but slightly brighter *H. macra* 'Aureola', is the classic grass to grow with blue-leaved hostas like 'Blue Angel', 'Halcyon', 'Love Pat' or the even larger *H. sieboldiana* var. *elegans*. Golden Hakone grass has several other cultivated forms and is tolerant of shade but equally happy in sun, and it is at ease in either heavy or light, acid or alkaline soils.

The tufted hair grass (*Deschampsia cespitosa*) is similarly adaptable to a wide variety of conditions and is one the few flowering grasses that excel in shade. The recently introduced *D. cespitosa* 'Northern Lights' is a very fine variegated grass that performs best in shade and in just the sort of rich, moist soils in which hostas luxuriate. Most sedges (see also 'Hostas with Ferns', p.49) and woodrushes grow best in shade, and again make ideal companions for hostas. The golden woodrush (*Luzula sylvatica* 'Aurea') is especially useful; its leaves are yellowish green through summer, and in winter they become vivid golden yellow.

Hostas in cottage gardens

The less brightly coloured hostas are the most suitable for planting in the style of old-fashioned cottage gardens. Here, annuals and perennials provide the colour, and hostas behave as a background. Columbines (*Aquilegia*) enjoy the same light shade as hostas, and with their complex, divided foliage, they act as a foil against the simple outlines of hosta leaves. Cultivars of *A. vulgaris*, such as the black-and-white-flowered 'William Guinness', 'Ruby Port' and 'Black Barlow' associate well with *Hosta lancifolia* or grey-green 'Snowden'. The yellow mottling of *Aquilegia vulgaris* Vervaeneana Group columbines, like 'Woodside', or the all-yellow-leaved 'Mellow Yellow', are more modern in effect and would make an excellent contrast for *Hosta* 'Sparkling Burgandy'. Once established, the columbines seed themselves around, coming up wherever they are happy, to give a relaxed, cottage-garden effect. Hostas can be preceded by cottage peonies, with their red leaf stalks and red-tinted leaves; these are past their best by early summer, leaving space for the burgeoning hosta leaves.

Later in summer, phloxes, though usually grown in the sun, will flourish among hostas. They are worth growing not only for the value of their relatively late flowers, but also for their architecture, which is radically different from that of hostas. The lavender-blue flowers of *Phlox paniculata* 'Blue Boy', 'Cool of the Evening' and 'Eventide' echo the mauve and purple shades of the hosta flowers, while the brasher orange-reds of 'Prince of Orange' or 'Brigadier' complement the pale yellow-green, lax foliage of *Hosta* 'Honeybells'.

A few foliage associations in cottage or country gardens can also work well. The tall-stemmed, bright glaucous sea-green, finely divided leaves of meadow rues (*Thalictrum*) provide a delicate tracery of leaves, and the spotted, rough-coated leaves of lungworts (*Pulmonaria*) provide a textural contrast to hostas. *P. saccharata* 'Leopard' also bears reddish pink flowers that provide late winter colour before the hostas emerge. Another plant valued for its foliage, which fits well into a cottage garden setting in light shade, is *Persicaria virginiana* 'Painter's Palette'. It makes a small perennial bush with masses of oval, chicken-egg-sized leaves marked and mottled cream, green and red with an inverted brown chevron right across the middle of each leaf. These are carried on red stems, and in late summer are joined by thin spikes of tiny white flowers followed by tiny red berries.

In a cottage garden, a clump of green-leaved hostas can be a perfect foil to wispy annuals and perennials.

Exotic effects in the shade

For those seeking a more exotic effect, the various ginger lilies (*Hedychium*) come into their own when grown with hostas, and several of them are reasonably frost hardy, most notably *Hedychium coronarium* with fragrant white flowers, *H. densiflorum* and its forms 'Assam Orange' and 'Stephen', and the yellow-flowered *H. forrestii* and *H. gardnerianum*. These all make good companions for the larger hostas, in sun or shade, because their form is totally different from that of hostas and they like to grow in the same conditions as regards to soil, moisture, feeding and light. Ginger lilies are inclined to overwhelm smaller hostas, but there are smaller ginger relatives such as cautleyas and roscoeas.

HOSTAS WITH BULBS

Early in the season before hostas come into leaf, an underplanting of bulbs adds considerable interest to any area largely devoted to hostas. Snowdrops (*Galanthus*) are especially useful since varieties can be chosen to flower from early winter until mid-spring. Smaller hostas are best underplanted with snowdrops, since both plants dislike animal manures and are happy with mulches of leafmould and garden compost.

Grape hyacinths (*Muscari*) with flowers in white or various shades of blue will usually seed themselves around or under the leaves of hostas. Lesser-known small bulbs that also thrive under the same conditions as hostas include scillas and the closely related pushkinias. The star of Bethlehem (*Ornithogalum nutans*) produces heads of ravishing green and white flowers in early summer, and then quickly dies away; be aware that in light, sandy soils it can become invasive. Lilies can also make good companions for hostas, because their form is so different from that of hostas. *Lilium martagon* is particularly apt, and there is a huge range of modern hybrid lilies to explore; these are generally easier to grow than the species.

HOSTAS IN THE SUN

Many hostas will perform well in sun provided that there is constant moisture available at their roots. If the soil dries out, the leaves will scorch at the edges and hostas will not attain their optimum size. *Hosta plantaginea*, the August lily of cottage gardens, is almost unique among hosta species in that it actually needs to be grown in sun, and flowers best at the foot of a sunny wall or in a conservatory. In temperate regions, its double-flowered forms 'Aphrodite' and 'Venus' will only produce their amazingly fragrant double white flowers if given the protection of glass but 'White Fairy' will sometimes flower outside if the summer is hot and it is given optimum conditions. In shade, *H. plantaginea* seldom flowers and the foliage becomes etiolated. Some yellow-leaved hostas also need to be grown in some sun to intensify their colouring. They also flower earlier and more freely in the sun. Among these are 'Aspen Gold', 'August Moon' and 'Little Aurora'.

In recent years, North American hosta breeders have crossed *H. plantaginea* with several other types of hosta to produce hardy, sun-tolerant varieties, mostly with flowers in shades of lilac. As *H. plantaginea* has powerfully and exotically fragrant flowers, a measure of fragrance has been passed on to its offspring. Among the best of these modern sun-tolerant hostas are: 'Royal Standard', which has white flowers similar to those of *H. plantaginea*, but smaller, and which has inherited much of its fragrance; 'Honeybells', which is less elegant with pale

A large planting of Hosta 'Royal Standard' *will scent the air on a warm summer evening.*

57

mauve flowers and light yellow-green leaves but has a rampant habit, making it ideal for ground cover in sun; 'Invincible' with thick, shining olive-green leaves and lightly fragrant mauve flowers; and 'Fragrant Bouquet' with variegated foliage. 'Sum and Substance' also has *H. plantaginea* in its ancestry, and it is outstanding among the larger sun-loving hostas, producing huge, heart-shaped leaves on very long stalks and heavy heads of pale flowers on leaning stems. In sun, the exceptionally thick

A bold hosta in a big pot draws the eye right into the heart of this mixed grouping.

leaves vary from old gold to bright yellow, while in shade they remain chartreuse. 'Sum and Substance' has produced several sports, the best of which is 'Lady Isobel Barnett' with cream-margined, light olive-green leaves.

All of these sun-tolerant hostas have the same soil, moisture and feeding needs as other hostas, and most flower in the second half of summer, so they make good companions for late-flowering perennials. Some stunning combinations can be achieved using yellow-leaved hostas like 'August Moon' with drifts of deep blue-flowered African blue lilies (*Agapanthus*) and orange-flowered montbretias (*Crocosmia*); these could be backed by striped zebra grasses (*Miscanthus sinensis* 'Strictus'), for example.

Sun-tolerant hostas

'Aspen Gold'	'Lady Isobel Barnett'
'August Moon'	'Midas Touch'
'Blue Umbrellas'	'Millie's Memoirs'
H. fortunei var.	*H. plantaginea* and forms
aureomarginata	'Potomac Pride'
'Fragrant Bouquet'	'Royal Standard'
'Honeybells'	'Sum and Substance'
'Invincible'	

HOSTAS IN CONTAINERS

The growing of hostas in containers is becoming increasingly popular, partly because the leaf mound of most hostas makes a very complementary shape to that of a typical garden pot or container. It also makes it easier to control damage by slugs and snails. On the whole, it is the medium-sized to large hostas that are most successful in pots, since very small and dwarf hostas generally need rather particular cultural conditions.

Before you decide which hostas to plant, consider where the containers are to be placed, whether in sun or shade, or in a windy or sheltered position, as this may affect the choice of hostas. While most hostas are usually treated as shade lovers, there are a number that will grow and perform well in sun and are often better for it, provided that adequate moisture is available at the roots. The size of the hosta and the size of the container should be in proportion; huge hostas need huge containers, and so on.

Also consider the aesthetic relationship between the hosta and the container in which it is to grow. As a rule of thumb, the more complex the variegation on the leaf of the hosta, the simpler the surface design of the pot should be, otherwise the patterns can clash. *Hosta* 'June', for example, has a very bright and contrasting blue-and-yellow variegation, which can look

positively jazzy in a large mound. Such a hosta is best grown in a simple container, but a hosta with plain green or blue leaves, such as 'Halcyon' or *H. ventricosa* could well be grown in a container whose surface is highly decorated – even in a ceramic pot patterned with rampant dragons! Sometimes, it may be worth matching the colour of the leaves, or one of the colours in the leaves, to the container. I grow 'Frances Williams' in an old brown Chinese egg-jar, which has a blue glaze around the lip that matches exactly the blue at the centre of that hosta's leaves.

The tiny-leaved Hosta 'Masquerade' is best grown in pots or sinks (as here) where it will not be swamped by larger hostas needing a different type of cultivation.

Furthermore, leaves of different sizes create different foliage effects. A single *H. sieboldiana* var. *elegans* in a large pot, for example, will produce relatively few, rather large, grey-blue leaves. Three 'Buckshaw Blue' hostas, however, would produce much the same grey-blue colouring, but the much greater number of much smaller leaves would create a quite different foliage effect.

Hostas on terraces and patios

Hostas in containers are as much at home on formal stone terraces as they are on tiny patios or in courtyards. Paving slabs, bricks and wooden decking are all suitable surfaces on which to grow hostas in containers, since hard landscaping materials and hostas always seem to enhance one another's appearance.

Contrary to Spanish tradition, a patio in England is now regarded as a paved area sited in as much sun as possible. Sun-tolerant hostas are the obvious choice here (see 'Hostas in the Sun', p.57), even though they may not have full sun throughout the day. They will still absorb a great deal of heat, however, especially if the area is enclosed to some extent, so regular watering in even more copious quantities than normal will be necessary. Large expanses of stone or brick terraces are often in full sun for most of the day, but they tend to be cooler than patios because more air and wind is present. 'Royal Standard' and *H. plantaginea* will revel in these sunny conditions and, as a bonus, their glorious fragrance will scent the evening air.

If part of the terrace or patio is in shade for some of the day, the range of hostas that can be grown is greatly extended. *H. fortunei* var. *aureomarginata* and its newly introduced sport 'Twilight' will thrive here, as will 'Mildred Seaver' and 'Wide Brim'.

The best hostas for growing in containers

'Francee'	'Masquerade'
'Frances Williams' (needs frequent dividing)	'Mildred Seaver'
	'Patriot'
'Gold Standard'	*H. plantaginea* var.
'Golden Tiara'	*japonica* (in sun)
'Green Fountain'	'Royal Standard' (in sun)
'Halcyon'	'Sum and Substance'
'June'	(in sun)
'Lady Isobel Barnett'	'Veronica Lake'
(in sun)	'Wide Brim'
H. lancifolia	

HOSTAS AT THE WATERSIDE

Hostas look superb growing beside water, especially on the banks of streams or at the edge of ponds. In gardens, two problems arise: the first is that most modern ponds are built from impermeable concrete or with plastic liners, so that the soil at the water's edge may be as dry as dust; and the second is that conventional wisdom states that hostas will not grow with their feet in still or stagnant water.

Although certain hosta species grow naturally in water meadows or with their roots in rushing streams, relatively little is known about which garden varieties will grow with their

roots in water, at least during the summer months. Experience, however, shows that 'Francee', *H. undulata*, *H. sieboldii* and their several forms will succeed when grown in pots standing in water, provided that the crown is kept above water level.

The problem of dry soil at the water's edge can be solved by digging copious quantities of well-rotted organic material into the soil, followed by the discreet positioning of a seep hose. Once the hostas are in growth, their leaves soon hide the hose, which can also be hidden under mulch. A more radical solution is to sink a leaky bucket (or several buckets) deep into the ground and plant hostas and other moisture-loving plants above it. Dig a hole big enough for the bucket, then punch one or two small holes through the bottom of the bucket and sink it in the hole so that its rim is at least 15cm (6in) below the soil surface. Finally, refill both the hole and the bucket with the removed soil. This will impede drainage sufficiently for the plants to flourish as well as they would if they were in genuinely moist soil.

Hosta fortunei *var.*
aureomarginata *is*
the dominant plant
in this tranquil
waterside planting.
Contrasting and
supporting foliage is
supplied by Iris
sibirica, *the fern*
Matteuccia
struthiopteris *and*
Carex elata, *a*
moisture loving sedge.

63

A SELECTION OF HOSTA SPECIES AND CULTIVARS

This list is a selection showing the diversity of hostas. It is by no means exhaustive and is designed to reveal the range of leaf shapes and colours to be found in hostas. Unless otherwise mentioned, the hostas described here form rounded mounds and have heart-shaped leaves. There is a considerable variety in the size of hostas, however, and the American Hosta Society defines the size of a hosta by the height of its foliage mound. This system is also used in many hosta catalogues and websites. These definitions are as follows:

Section	Size
1 Giant	*over 70cm (28in)*
2 Large	*45-70cm (18-28in)*
3 Medium	*25-45cm (10-18in)*
4 Small	*15-25cm (6-10in)*
5 Miniature	*10-15cm (4-6in)*
4 Dwarf	*up to 10cm (4in)*

The spread of hostas is defined as the diameter of the leaf mound, and this varies according to climate, cultivation and soil conditions. Most hostas are hardy to frost and need light to dappled shade (see 'How to Grow Hostas', p.18). If a hosta is known to need more light or more shade, this is stated.

The main flowering season for hostas is late June to early July in southern England, and this is referred to as mid-season in the following list; naturally, early- and late-season flowers appear just before or after these dates. For those gardening further north, allow for a one-week delay per 160km (100 miles) travelled north from the south coast, and a similar delay every 30m (100ft) increase in altitude, depending on microclimate. For those gardening in other countries, mid-season here is the three or four weeks following the summer solstice. Further south, in continental Europe, hostas flower only marginally earlier than the UK, and apart from *H. plantaginea* and some of its hybrids, few hostas grow well in Mediterranean climates. The flower scapes are measured by their length.

'Abiqua Moonbeam' needs some sun to colour well and enough moisture to produce puckering on the leaf surfaces.

'Abiqua Moonbeam'
Medium to large green and yellow leaves making a colourful mound. Leaves: oval to heart-shaped, the base folded into the navel, corrugation present when mature, mid-green with a wide, irregular chartreuse to yellow margin. The variegation is

barely present when the leaves unfurl, but gradually becomes more pronounced. Colours best in some sun. Flowers: mid-season, very pale lavender on 60cm (24in) stems. One of the many worthwhile sports of the classic yellow-leaved 'August Moon'. Spread: 75cm (30in). Height: 50cm (20in).

'Aspen Gold'
Slug resistant, medium to large corrugated yellow leaves. Leaves: nearly round, heart-shaped at the base, lobes folded at the navel, thick, strongly cup-shaped, intensely corrugated, unfurling chartreuse, becoming golden-yellow with a light surface bloom by late summer. Flowers: mid-season, funnel-shaped, palest lavender to nearly white, carried on straight, leafy stems, barely overtopping the foliage. Colours best in some sun. 'Millie's Memoirs' is a recently introduced sport with green centred leaves. Spread: 90cm (36in). Height: 50cm (20in).

'Blue Angel'
Giant, vigorous, grey-blue hosta of architectural habit. Leaves: huge, oval to heart-shaped with a conspicuously lobed base, matt surface texture with pronounced veining, slightly wavy at the margins pointed at the tip, grey rather than blue, the blade held at right angles to the leaf-stalk. Attractive spikes of pale mauve to nearly white funnel-shaped flowers in mid-season on 120cm (48in) bare stems. A sumptuous hosta when well grown, but takes a few years to mature. Superb amongst other green-leaved or yellow-leaved hostas, but its leaf colour is diminished when grown beside bluer-leaved hostas such as the much slower-growing *H.* 'Big Daddy'. Spread: 210cm (83in). Height up to 90cm (36in).

'Blue Arrow'
Distinct among medium-sized blue hostas for its unique upright habit and elegant leaf shape. Leaves: medium-sized, rich blue, arrow-shaped. Slightly cupped, triangular or narrowly triangular, blade slightly wavy, nearly square at the base. Flowers: mid-season, funnel-shaped, palest lavender to nearly white, borne on straight, bare 45cm (18in) stems. Valued for its slug resistant qualities. Spread: 45cm (18in). Height: 25cm (10in).

The relatively slug-of, rich blue leaves of Hosta 'Blue Arrow' are shaped like arrowheads.

'Blue Moon'

Small, slow-growing, blue-leaved hosta. Leaves: dwarf, rounded to heart-shaped, thick, leathery, slightly cupped, slightly puckered, rich blue. Flowers: mid-season, funnel-shaped, palest lavender-grey on 30cm (12in) stems. Sometimes confused in the trade with 'Dorset Blue', which is larger in all its parts. One of the smallest blue-leaved hostas. 'Blue Ice' ('Dorset Blue' × 'Blue Moon') is smaller but a less intense blue. Spread: 25cm (10in). Height: up to 20cm (8in).

'Borwick Beauty'

Sumptuous and showy large blue-and-yellow-leaved hosta. Leaves: round to heart-shaped, conspicuously lobed and folded into the navel, deeply puckered when mature, blue with a large creamy yellow central area, with some streaking into the margins. Flowers: mid-season, narrowly funnel-shaped, nearly white or palest lavender on straight, leafy stems borne just above the foliage mound. *H.* 'Color Glory' is considered identical, *H.* 'George Smith' and *H.* 'Great Expectations' are similar. All increase slowly and need constant dappled shade as leaves tend to scorch in sun. Spread: 150cm (60in). Height: 60cm (24in).

'Camelot'
Medium-sized hosta prized for its exceptional light blue foliage. Leaves: medium, heart-shaped to rounded, thick, slightly puckered, intensely bright pale blue. Flowers: mid-season, funnel-shaped, palest lavender to almost white on 38cm (15in) straight, bare, stems. Will take more shade than most. Spread: 55cm (22in). Height: 38cm (15in).

'Cherry Berry'
Eye-catching, small green and white narrow-leaved hosta with showy, bright purple flowers. Leaves: narrow, downward curving, slightly shiny, white-centred with irregular dark green margins of thin substance carried on reddish stalks. Flowers: mid-season to late, funnel-shaped, carried on straight, bare, bright red stems, the flowers being followed by red seed pods. A delightful hosta grown for both leaves and flowers.

Hosta 'Camelot' is a little-known, but outstanding, hosta having distinctive frosty, pale blue leaves with a strongly marked surface texture.

H. 'Maraschino Cherry' is an attractive dark green-leaved sport. Needs some morning sun and good light to maintain vigour. Spread: 60cm (24in). Height: 30cm (12in).

'Chôkô Nishiki' (syn. 'On Stage')

Large cream to yellow centrally variegated hosta. Leaves: large, widely oval, ribbed, shiny, the centre bright yellow-gold on unfurling, becoming creamy chartreuse later with a rich green margin randomly streaking into the blade. Flowers: mid-season, funnel-shaped, pale lavender on leaning, bare 75cm (30in) stems. One of the most distinct hostas but slow to make big clumps. Needs morning sun to produce the bright colour. Leaves: emerge later in spring than those of *H. montana* 'Aureomarginata' to which it is closely related, and so usually escape frost damage. Spread: 90cm (36in). Height 50cm (20in).

'Christmas Tree'

Large, rounded, yellow to creamy white and green hosta. Leaves: round to heart-shaped, the veins deeply impressed, the lobes folded into the navel, the surface covered with a grey-blue bloom and somewhat puckered, mid- to dark green, the margin narrow and irregularly variegated yellow to creamy white. Flowers: mid-season, funnel-shaped, on straight, leafy stems 45cm (18in) tall. The seedpods are a distinctive aubergine colour. *H.* 'Christmas Tree Gala' is a streaked sport much used

Hosta 'Cherry Berry', in common with many thin-leafed, white-centred hostas, can be tricky to site in the garden.

for breeding new hostas. Spread: 140cm (55in). Height: 55cm (22in).

'Daybreak'

Large bright golden-yellow-leaved hosta. Leaves: wedge-shaped to heart-shaped, the blade slightly wavy, the tip turned down, green at first becoming shiny, bright yellow. The leaf stalks surprisingly short for the length of the blade. Flowers: large racemes of flowers mid-season to late, funnel-shaped, lavender, on straight, bare stems up to nearly 90cm (36in), which droop onto the foliage. Colours best in light shade. *H.* 'Day's End' is a recently introduced green-centred sport. Spread: 150cm (60in). Height: 60cm (24in).

'Devon Green'

Shapely, medium-sized, glossy green-leaved hosta. Leaves: near oval in the juvenile state, becoming elegantly heart-shaped at maturity; prominently-veined, thick, glossy, rich dark green. Mahogany-tinted leaf stalks and flower stems make an attractive contrast. Flowers: dense raceme of somewhat bell-shaped greyish lavender flowers, followed by an abundance of seedpods. A striking sport of *H.* 'Halcyon', the best-known of the Tardiana Group. *H.* 'Peridot' and *H.* 'Valerie's Vanity' are similar. Spread: 90cm (36in). Height: 45cm (18in).

'Donahue Piecrust'

Large green-leaved hosta with rippled margins. Leaves: oval to near heart-shaped, tapering to a point, margins tightly rippled, moderately lobed, conspicuously veined, mid-green. Flowers: mid-season, bell-shaped, pale lavender, on 85cm (34in) leaning stems. An excellent parent for 'piecrust'-leaved hostas. Spread: 120cm (48in). Height: 60cm (24in).

'Emerald Tiara'

Small to medium-sized, green- and yellow-leaved hosta. Leaves: compact clump of widely oval, thin, smooth, satiny yellow to cream leaves very irregularly margined, rich green. Flowers: dense racemes of bell-shaped, purple flowers on 75cm (30in) stems in mid- to late summer. One of the best sports of the classic

H. 'Golden Tiara', the more evenly shaped leaves making a very graceful and attractive mound. Best in dappled shade but will tolerate morning sun, although the leaf colours tend to fade. Spread: 75cm (30in). Height: 38cm (15in).

'Fire and Ice'

Small to medium-sized striking green-and-white hosta. Leaves: erect mound of upwardly pointing pure white leaves encircled by an irregular margin of dark green. Flowers: pale lavender on sturdy, 45cm (18in) leafy stems in mid- to late summer. Needs morning sun or light dappled shade to maintain its vigour. One of the many sports of *H.* 'Patriot'. *H.* 'Loyalist' is similar and *H.* 'Revolution' has white-centred leaves overlaid with a fine green misting. All are ultimately smaller than *H.* 'Patriot'. Spread: 38cm (15in). Height: 25cm (10in).

Hosta fortunei var. *albopicta*

Medium to large classic hosta with striking creamy yellow central viridescent variegation. Leaves: oval to near heart-shaped, unfurling pale yellow with an irregular, deep green margin and some streaking where the yellow and green overlap; attractive veining. The leaves only have a shadowy hint of variegation by flowering time. Flowers: mid-season,

The slow-growing, but eye-catching, Hosta *'Fire and Ice' needs good light and a little direct morning sun to give of its best.*

funnel-shaped, lavender, on straight, leafy stems to 90cm (36in). One of the most colourful of all hardy perennial plants in early summer. Its sport, *H. fortunei* var. *albopicta* f. *aurea*, one of the earliest of the golden-yellow-leaved hostas and once very popular, has been superseded by hostas which retain their colour all season. Spread: 120cm (48in). Height: 50cm (20in).

'Fragrant Bouquet'
Lightly fragrant-flowered, white-margined hosta. Leaves: medium-large, oval to almost heart-shaped, of good substance, the blade slightly wavy, light green to chartreuse with an irregular creamy white margin. Flowers: late, large, widely funnel-shaped, fragrant, palest lavender to near white on straight stems to 90cm (36in), the stems bearing a single large, twisted and variegated leafy bract just below the flowers. Thrives in sun or a little shade and increases rapidly. *H.* 'Guacamole' is a sport with muted variegation, which has now produced its own mutation, 'Stained Glass', with much bolder variegation. Spread: 120cm (48in). Height: 55cm (22in).

'Francee'
Classic large green-and-white-leaved hosta ideal for mass planting. Leaves: emerge later than most, narrowly heart-shaped, slightly lobed, mid- to dark green with an irregular, clean white margin. Flowers: mid-season, funnel-shaped, on leaning, leafy stems to 75cm (30in). One of the most attractive of the white-edged hostas and a good performer under varied conditions. Best in light shade and excellent in pots and containers. *H.* 'Patriot' and *H.* 'Minuteman' are well-known sports. Spread: 120cm (48in). Height: 60cm (24in).

'Frances Williams'
Large to giant blue-and-yellow-leaved hosta. Leaves: rounded to heart-shaped, deeply lobed, stiff, thick, corrugated, rich powdery blue with a broad, irregular yellow to beige margin. Flowers: mid-season, funnel-shaped, palest lavender to near-white, densely packed at the top of leafy stems, the stem leaves being conspicuous and variegated like the leaves, the flowers only just overtopping the leaf mound. Must be sited out of

Hosta *'Frosted Jade'* is one of the very best of the giant-leaved variegated hostas.

direct sunlight to prevent leaf scorch. *H.* 'Samurai' and *H.* 'Aurora Borealis' are similar and can also suffer from leaf scorch but *H.* 'Olive Bailey Langdon' is similar and suffers much less from scorch damage. Spread: 150cm (60in). Height: 70cm (28in).

'Frosted Jade'

Giant green and white hosta with a distinctive upright and arching habit. Leaves: oval, tapering to the tip, furrowed, slightly rippled edges causing distinctive upward cupping, mid-green with clear white margins sometimes streaking towards the green leaf centre. Flowers: mid-season, funnel-shaped, nearly white or palest lavender on leaning leafy stems, the stem leaves also attractively variegated. Needs shade. The similar *H.* 'Mountain Snow' is closely related but has bolder variegation. Spread: 150cm (60in). Height: 75cm (30in).

'Ginko Craig'

Medium-sized, white-margined, groundcover hosta. Leaves: narrow, turning under at the tip, slightly wavy edge, matt dark green, narrowly margined in white with slight streaking into the centre. Leaves on mature clumps become longer and the margin wider. Flowers: late, funnel-shaped, purple, on straight, bare stems to 45cm (18in). Needs shade. Forms drifts rather than clumps and has a loosely running root structure. Spread: 100cm (40in). Height: 25–45cm (10–18in).

'Gold Standard'

Large, fast-growing lutescent green-and-gold-leaved hosta. Leaves: oval to heart-shaped, lobes rounded, chartreuse at first becoming bright yellow, finally fading to an attractive ivory-parchment, with wide, irregular dark green margins. Flowers: mid-season, funnel-shaped, lavender on straight, bare stems to 105cm (42in). One of the most popular and attractive of all hostas but needs to be carefully placed. In too much shade the leaf centre remains light green, while in too much sun the variegation bleaches out to white or actually scorches. Needs good cultivation and plenty of moisture. A versatile container specimen. Spread: 150cm (60in). Height: 50cm (20in).

The glossy, dark green leaves of Hosta 'Devon Green', a superb sport of H. 'Halcyon', are enhanced by its mahogany-tinted flower and leaf stems. It is equally as good in a pot as in a border.

'Golden Tiara'

Medium, rapidly-increasing green-and-yellow-leaved hosta. Leaves: small on long leaf stalks, the inner leaves heart-shaped to almost round, the outer ones almost oval, mid-green with a broad margin of chartreuse turning creamy yellow. Flowers: mid- to late season, funnel-shaped, rich lavender-purple on straight, bare stems to 75cm (30in). One of the very best small to medium sized hostas, of neat, compact and dense habit, the leaves overlapping like fish scales. The first of the 'Tiara' series. Others include white-margined *H.* 'Diamond Tiara', *H.* 'Emerald Tiara', *H.* 'Golden Scepter' with entirely gold leaves, *H.* 'Grand Prize', which has yellow marginal variegation turning white; and *H.* 'Grand Tiara' which has much wider marginal variegation. All make excellent container specimens. Spread: 90cm (36in). Height: 38cm (15in).

'Green Fountain'

Large, green hosta forming a cascading mound. Leaves: narrow, the edges rippled, the tip twisted, the veins conspicuous, smooth, mid-green, the leaf stalk dotted red. Flowers: mid-season to late, funnel-shaped, rich lavender on leaning, red-streaked leafy stems to 90cm (36in), stem leaves most conspicuous just below flowers. Distinct among green-leaved hostas for its cascading leaf habit. A most attractive hosta for tall pots and containers. Spread: 120cm (48in). Height: 60cm (24in).

'Halcyon'

Classic, medium, blue-leaved hosta. Leaves: oval in juvenile plants, heart-shaped on maturity, narrowly lobed, thick, flat, smooth, rich blue, making a pleasing symmetrical mound. Flowers: mid-season, bell-shaped, greyish lavender to nearly white in dense spikes on straight, mauve-grey, bare stems to 60cm (24in). One of the best blue-leaved hostas, intensely blue in deeper shade. Wonderful in shiny blue or green ceramic pots. The best-known offspring of the series of small to medium-sized leaved powdery blue hostas raised from a cross between *H. sieboldiana* var. *alba* and the late-flowering *H. tardiflora*. Spread: 90cm (36in). Height: 50cm (20in).

'Invincible'

Sun-tolerant, medium-sized, leathery green-leaved hosta. Leaves: wedge-shaped tapering to a long point, the blade wavy, leathery, slightly shiny, dark olive-green, the stems dotted red. Flowers lightly fragrant, late, funnel-shaped and occasionally double (hose-in-hose), pale lavender on leaning, leafy stems to 50cm (20in) stained red in patches. One of the smaller *H. plantaginea* hybrids of compact and pleasing habit. Reasonably slug and snail proof. Spread: 100cm (40in). Height: 38cm (15in).

'Jade Cascade'

Giant, green-leaved hosta making a sumptuous cascading mound. Leaves: immense, narrowly wedge-shaped, tapering to a graceful tip, deeply furrowed, the leaf stalks upright, as much as 75cm (30in) tall, the blade of the leaf pendulous. Flowers: mid-season to late, funnel-shaped, on leaning, leafy stems to 120cm (48in). Slow to mature but ultimately one of the very largest hostas. Spread: 180cm (72in). Height: 90cm (36in).

'June'

Colourful, medium-sized blue-and-yellow-leaved hosta. Leaves: oval on juvenile plants, heart-shaped at maturity, thick, flat, smooth chartreuse to yellow with an irregular blue-green margin, the blue-green and yellow overlapping and streaking to produce a colourful blend of tonal harmony. Flowers: mid-season, bell-shaped, greyish lavender borne densely on straight, bare stems to 60cm (24in). Needs good light or morning sun to produce the strongest colouring, but is more muted if grown in shade. The best-known sport of *H.* 'Halcyon'. Spread: 100cm (40in). Height: 38cm (15in).

Hosta *'June'* has a more muted variegation when grown in shade (as here). In good light or in some sun, the leaves become much brighter.

'Just So'
Small yellow-and-green-leaved hosta. Leaves: oval to nearly heart-shaped, lobes rounded, thick, cupped, puckered, chartreuse to bright yellow, the narrow dark green margin streaking randomly into the yellow centre. Flowers: mid-season, funnel-shaped, pale lavender on straight, leafy stems to 30cm (12in) tall. A colourful hosta for the lightly shaded rock garden. Spread: 60cm (24in). Height: 20cm (8in).

'Krossa Regal'
Giant blue-grey hosta of unique poise. Leaves: narrowly wedge-shaped, blade wavy, powdery greyish blue-green carried on long, upright leaf stalks. Flowers: mid-season, funnel-shaped, lavender on tall, undulating bare, powdery pale bluish green stems up to 140cm (55in). Distinct among hostas for its clump of vase-shaped foliage. Light shade. *H.* 'Regal Splendor' is an eye-catching cream-margined sport. Spread: 180cm (72in). Height: 75cm (30in).

'Lakeside Black Satin'
Large sized very dark green-leaved hosta. Leaves: heart-shaped, deeply lobed, rippled edges, widely-veined, thin, glossy, darkest green. Flowers: late, distinctly bell-shaped, deep purple striped white on stems to 65cm (26in). Has the darkest green leaves of

Hosta *'Just So'* is a pretty and colourful plant that thrives in lightly shaded borders and rock gardens.

any hosta, appearing almost black in some conditions. A seedling of, and very similar to, *H. ventricosa*. Light to full shade. Spread: 120cm (48in). Height: 50cm (20in).

'Lakeside Symphony'
Large, yellow-leaved hosta with a muted chartreuse margin. Leaves: oval to wedge-shaped, edges slightly rippled producing a somewhat concave effect, deeply lobed, blade wavy, thick, some puckering between the well-marked veins, golden-yellow margins. Flowers: mid-season, bell-shaped, pale lavender flowers on straight, bare stems to 80cm (32in). Sport of the golden-leaved *H.* 'Sun Power'. *H.* 'Paradise Power' is similar. Spread: 150cm (60in). Height: 60cm (24in).

Hosta lancifolia
Medium-size, classic, green hosta making a graceful mound. Leaves: narrow, pointed at the tip, thin, shiny dark green above, paler beneath, the leaf stalk long and red spotted towards the base. Flowers: late, funnel-shaped, purple on leaning, leafy stems to 60cm (24in). Useful for its late flowering and for its spreading habit, making large drifts in time. Excellent ground cover and lovely in wooden containers. Probably not a true species as originally designated. Spread: 90cm (36in). Height: 38cm (15in).

'Little Aurora'

Small, gold-leaved hosta making a dense mound. Leaves: heart-shaped, deeply lobed, cupped and closed at the navel, thick, puckered, bright golden-yellow, which holds its colour well in shade. Flowers: mid-season, bell-shaped, palest lavender to near white, on straight, bare stems to 30cm (12in). One of the best smallish gold hostas. Worthwhile sports include the slow-growing, green-leaved, yellow-margined *H.* 'Sultana'; the gold centred, very dark green-margined *H.* 'Little Sunspot'. Confused in the trade with *H.* 'Golden Prayers', whose larger leaves have a more upright habit. Spread: 60cm (24in). Height: 20cm (8in).

Hosta longissima

Medium hosta forming dense mounds of very narrow green leaves. Leaves: narrow, gracefully pointed, matt, mid-green. Flowers: late, funnel-shaped, reddish purple, on 40cm (16in) leafy stems. Must have moisture at its roots. Seen less often in gardens now than its hybrid, *H.* 'Purple Lady Finger'. Spread: 60cm (24in). Height: 30cm (12in).

'Love Pat'

Large hosta with intensely blue, cupped leaves. Leaves stiff, thick, almost round, deeply lobed, very cupped and very puckered. Flowers: mid-season, bell-shaped on straight, bare stems to 62cm (25in). A lovely hosta needing a position in shade but open to the sky. Under trees its upturned leaves will collect falling twigs thus spoiling the attractively seersuckered leaf surface. A larger and much faster-growing hybrid of *H. tokudama*, which, with its variegated sports, is known to be slow to increase. Spread: 90cm (36in). Height: 50cm (20in).

'Masquerade'

The golden-yellow leaves of Hosta *'Lakeside Symphony' have a shadowy lime-green marginal variegation.*

Miniature green- and white-leaved hosta making an upright mound. Leaves: narrow, thin, white at first with a dark green margin, sometimes turning pale green later. Flowers: funnel-shaped, lavender with purple stripes on straight, leafy stems. Delightful, strongly variegated hosta best grown in shade. Although requiring careful cultivation, it is ideal for the shaded rock garden, peat bed or small containers. Occasionally produces tufts of larger, all-green leaves, which should be removed. Spread: 45cm (18in). Height: 15cm (6in).

'Mildred Seaver'

Large green-and-cream-leaved hosta of pleasing proportions. Leaves: medium to large, of good substance, oval to heart-shaped, puckered, green with a wide, irregular yellow to creamy white margin. Flowers: mid-season, funnel-shaped, pale lavender on straight, variegated leafy stems to 60cm (24in). Spread: 150cm (60in). Height: up to 60cm (24in).

Hosta montana 'Aureomarginata'

Large, spectacular yellow-edged green hosta making a cascading mound. Leaves: arching, oval to narrowly heart-shaped, drawn out to a point, markedly lobed, deeply furrowed, shiny mid-green with a broad, variable golden-yellow margin. Flowers: mid-season, funnel-shaped, palest lavender on pendulous, 100cm (40in) leafy stems. One of the showiest of hostas, the variegation positively dramatic, and grown to best advantage in a shaded shrub border or as a specimen in a woodland garden. Usually the first hosta into leaf in the spring, new leaves are often caught by frosts. If damaged leaves are removed the second flush will usually escape frost damage. Alternatively protect with horticultural fleece. Spread: 150cm (60in). Height 60cm (24in).

'Moonlight'

Large hosta with leaves in shades of chartreuse, yellow and white. Leaves: widely oval, the tip turned under, slightly puckered in mature clumps, emerging mid- to pale green, gradually changing through the season to rich golden yellow, finally fading to ivory parchment, edged with a narrow, irregular white margin. Flowers: mid-season, funnel-shaped, lavender, on straight, bare stems to 90cm (36in) tall. Ethereally beautiful hosta but not the easiest to place, requiring clear light out of direct sunlight or light shade. Worth every effort to site correctly. Spread: 120cm (48in). Height: 50cm (20in).

'Moon River'
Attractive, small, dense mound of green and white leaves. Leaves: oval to almost round, gracefully pointed at the tip, slightly puckered when mature, blue-green, broad and irregular margins of creamy white to white. Flowers: midsummer, near bell-shaped, lavender, on straight, bare stems 50cm (20in) tall. Makes a colourful specimen hosta for the front of the border. Spread: 65cm (26in). Height: 25cm (10in).

'Northern Exposure'
Large, dramatically variegated green and white hosta. Leaves: broadly oval to heart-shaped, deeply lobed and folded into the navel, margin slightly wavy, thick, very puckered dark blue-green, boldly and irregularly margined creamy white to white. Flowers: mid-summer, bell-shaped, greyish white on 70cm (28in) straight, leafy stems. Does not develop spring leaf scorch as do many of this type, thus giving more planting opportunities, although it colours best in dappled shade. Spread: 150cm (60in). Height: 65cm (26in).

The chartreuse margins of Hosta *'Mildred Seaver' become creamy white as the season advances.*

'Olive Branch'
Medium hosta with unusual leaf markings forming dense mounds. Leaves: almost round with a heart-shaped base carried on long leaf stalks, thin, satiny, muted butterscotch yellow,

widely margined dark green. Flowers: mid-season, funnel-shaped, purple, on straight, bare 50cm (20in) stems. A charming little hosta of unique colouring and great freedom of flower. Spread: 60cm (24in). Height: 35cm (14in).

Hosta opipara

Large yellow-and-green-leaved hosta. Leaves: narrowly oval, wavy, dark green with an irregular margin that is yellow at first, holding its colour reasonably well in shade but fading to near white in sun. Flowers: late, funnel-shaped, rich purple, on leaning, leafy 75cm (30in) stems. An interesting hosta with a loosely running root system, dramatic when grown in shade, and good in flower. Spread: 50cm (20in). Height: 50cm (20in).

'Patriot'

Boldly white-margined, large hosta. Leaves: oval to heart-shaped, gracefully pointed, slightly cupped and somewhat

puckered when mature, dark green with a contrasting wide margin, creamy white at first turning pure white. Flowers: mid-season, funnel-shaped, lavender on 75cm (30in) stems. A sport of *H.* 'Francee', from which it differs in its wider margin and slightly smaller size. *H.* 'Minuteman' is similar. Spread: 125cm (50in). Height: 58cm (23in) wide.

'Paul's Glory'
Large, yellow-leaved hosta with a blue-green margin. Leaves: oval to heart-shaped, deeply lobed and folded into the navel, puckered on mature plants, pale chartreuse on unfurling, becoming bright yellow with a narrow, dark blue margin, which turns dark green. Flowers: mid-season, bell-shaped, palest lavender, on straight, bare scapes to 90cm (36in) tall. Eye-catching and opulent. Best in light shade. Spread: 120cm (48in). Height: 60cm (24in).

'Queen Josephine'

Hosta opipara is a spreading hosta which is eye-catching in both leaf and flower.

Medium hosta with dark green, yellow-margined leaves. Leaves: oval to nearly heart-shaped, slightly lobed, thick, glossy rich dark green. Widely and evenly margined, yellow becoming white. Flowers: mid-season, funnel-shaped on straight, leafy stems to 60cm (24in). Suitable as a specimen plant or for container growing. Increases rapidly. Spread: 90cm (36in). Height: 40cm (16in).

'Royal Standard'
Large, green hosta with fragrant white flowers. Leaves: large, oval or narrowly heart-shaped, slightly wavy at the margin, shiny bright green. Flowers: funnel-shaped, opening pure white from palest lilac buds, occasionally double, on straight, leafy stems to 90cm (36in). By far the best white-flowered hosta around, easy to grow, happy in sun provided the roots are damp enough, rapidly making large clumps and filling the air with fragrance when planted in bold drifts. The closely-related *H.* 'Honeybells' is a coarser plant but has proven landscape uses. Spread: 120cm (48in). Height: 50cm (20in).

'Sagae'

Giant hosta with green leaves edged and streaked creamy yellow. Leaves: oval to triangular, deeply lobed, shallowly undulate, held horizontally on strong, upright leaf stalks, widely spaced veins, dark green, irregularly margined yellow to cream with grey streaking into the centre. Dense racemes of flowers mid- to late season, bell-shaped on leaning, leafy stems to 100cm (40in). Dappled shade. This superb hosta makes a spectacular vase-shaped mound. Spread: 180cm (72in). Height: 90cm (36in).

Hosta sieboldiana var. *elegans*

Giant, sumptuous, classic hosta with heavily puckered, powdery blue leaves. Leaves: heart-shaped to almost round, deeply lobed, very thick, deeply seersuckered in mature plants, taking on luminous yellow tones when frosted in autumn. Flowers: early to mid-season, funnel-shaped on straight leafy stems that scarcely rise above the foliage. It needs plenty of space and plenty of water and holds its colour best in light shade. The blueness of the leaves is produced by a thin coating of wax, and if planted near a path where the leaves are frequently brushed against by passers-by it will lose its blueness revealing the dark green beneath. Very fertile and the parent of attractive and sought-after introductions. Its instability in mature clumps has produced many gold-leaved sports, (*H.* 'Golden Sunburst') and variegated sports (*H.* 'Frances Williams'). Spread: 180cm (72in). Height: 75cm (30in).

Hosta *'So Sweet'* was awarded Hosta of the Year by the American Hosta Growers Association .

Hosta sieboldii

White-margined, narrow-leaved, medium species hosta. Leaves: narrow to near oval when mature, thin, matt dark green, narrowly margined bright white. Flowers: late, widely funnel-shaped purple, on 50cm (20in) leafy stems. Usually only seen now in older plantings as it has been superseded in gardens by a number of excellent hybrids, for example: *H.* 'Carrie Ann', white-margined with white flowers; *H.* 'Beatrice' and *H.* 'Neat Splash', both much used in current breeding programmes; *H.* 'Weihenstephan', is a selected form of *H. sieboldii* var. *alba* with green leaves and larger white flowers. Can cope with quite dry or very wet conditions. Spread: 90cm (36in). Height: 30cm (12in).

'Snowden'

Stately, giant, grey-blue hosta. Leaves: oval to narrowly heart-shaped, shallowly undulate, soft, green-tinged, grey-blue. Flowers: early to mid-season, bell-shaped, pale mauve on straight, bare stems to 95cm (38in) tall. Differs from other large grey-blue hostas of *H. sieboldiana* ancestry in its decidedly grey, not blue, colouring and in its narrower, more pointed leaves. Spread: 130cm (52in). Height: 80cm (32in).

'So Sweet'

Large, white-margined hosta with fragrant flowers. Leaves: narrowly oval with slightly wavy margins, of average substance, shiny, carried on very long leaf stalks, the yellow to creamy white variegation running down the wings of the leaf stalks. Flowers: late, widely funnel-shaped, pale lavender on 55cm (22in) stems. A pretty and useful hosta that flowers best in sun given enough moisture at its roots, the fragrance pervasive when several plants are grown in a group. Spread: 120cm (48in). Height: 45cm (18in).

'Sparkling Burgundy'

Medium-sized, green-leaved hosta grown mainly for its burgundy leaf stems and flower stalks. Leaves: narrowly oval, dark green, thick and glossy carried on long, burgundy-brown leaf stems. Flowers: mid-season to late, widely funnel-shaped, deep mauve flowers on straight, bare, burgundy-brown stems. The abundant flowers borne on dense racemes, are a wonderful sight when grown in drifts. Spread: 75cm (30in). Height: 38cm (15in).

'Stiletto'

Medium, spreading hosta with prettily rippled, white-margined leaves. Leaves: narrow, graduated at the tip, the edges strongly rippled on young plants, wavy on mature plants, thin, satiny, mid-green, margins cream fading to white. Flowers mid-season to late, funnel-shaped on straight leafy stems to 50cm (20in). Has a dense, mounding habit suitable for foreground planting, but also works well in pots and containers. Spread: 75cm (30in). Height: 30cm (12in).

Hosta 'Striptease' - a hosta with an entirely new sort of variegation. It will need dividing every few years to retain the narrow white lines and wide lime-green of the leaves.

'Striptease'

Outstanding large hosta with unusual white markings. Leaves: more oval than heart-shaped, slightly wavy at the edges, with a wide band of lime-green to yellow down the centre, outlined with white lines or flecks, surrounded by an even, dark green margin. Flowers: mid-season, funnel-shaped, lavender on straight, bare, 60cm (24in) stems. A new break in hosta variegation, giving *H.* 'Striptease' great appeal as a specimen plant. Spread: 120cm (48in). Height: 45cm (18in).

'Sum and Substance'

Giant, impressive hosta with chartreuse to yellow leaves. Leaves very large, blade wavy, deeply lobed, oval to heart-shaped, slightly cupped, very thick, satiny smooth on young plants but lightly puckered when mature, the leaves carried on long leaf stalks. Flowers: mid-season to late, bell-shaped on leaning, leafy, serpentine stems up to 100cm (40in) long. An immense hosta needing plenty of space and plenty of water at the roots, chartreuse in shade, increasingly yellow in more light but always an understated yellow. 'Lady Isobel Barnett' is a sport with a light olive-green centre and cream margin. 'Domaine de Courson' is a sport with dark olive-green leaves. Spread: 180cm (72in). Height: 90cm (36in).

'Summer Music'

Large hosta with white, centrally-variegated leaves. Leaves: oval to heart-shaped, tapering to a point, blade wavy, smooth on young plants, puckered when mature, ivory-white with very broad, light green to chartreuse margins. Flowers: mid-season, bell-shaped, pale lavender on 60cm (24in) leafy white stems. A strong grower for a hosta with a white central variegation. Needs dappled shade and plenty of moisture. Spread: 90cm (36in). Height: 40cm (16in).

'Twilight'

Large hosta with widely yellow-margined leaves. Leaves: oval to heart-shaped, markedly veined, with slight corrugation on mature plants, very thick, glossy, very dark green, evenly margined yellow. Flowers: mid-season, funnel-shaped, pale lavender, gathered towards the top of short, stout stems to about 60cm (24in) tall. Sport of the ever-popular *H. fortunei* var. *aureomarginata*, with thicker leaves and wider yellow margins. Spread: 120cm (48in). Height: 45cm (18in).

Hosta undulata var. *undulata*

Medium-sized hosta with dazzling white-centred, attractively twisted leaves. Leaves: narrowly oval, curled under at tip, the blade strongly twisted, thin, ivory- to pure-white, the variegation running down the leaf stalks, dark green irregular margins. Flowers: early to mid-season, funnel-shaped, lavender on straight, very leafy near-white stems, the flower stems and stem leaves also variegated. The first flush of leaves in spring are as described above but the second flush in the summer are less strongly variegated, the centres of the leaves being streaked and mottled green. Over the years the variegation tends to become narrower and the margin wider. Needs to be lifted and divided every three or four years to maintain its striking variegation. If the clumps are left undivided they mutate to *H. undulata* var. *univittata* having a very narrow central variegation and finally becoming a green-leaved form, *H. undulata* var. *erromena*. Two hours of morning sun then shade. Spread: 75cm (30in). Height: 25cm (10in).

'Urajiro' (*hypoleuca*)

Giant, white-backed hosta. Leaves: broadly oval with a curling tip, the margins rippled, matt, light green above, intensely white beneath, the leaf stalks heavily red spotted towards the base. Dense spikes of flowers mid- to late season, bell-shaped, mauve to almost white on leaning, leafy stalks to 60cm (24in), the stems red-dotted and streaked towards the base. Grows in the wild on volcanic cliff faces in Japan, in single leaf clumps, and is said to have developed the white powdery coating to the underside of its leaves as a defence against the intense heat reflected from the rocks. Best grown in an elevated position so that the backs of the leaves can be seen. Sun to light shade. *H.* 'Azure Snow' is a hybrid with rippled-edged, powdery light turquoise-blue leaves. The smaller, but somewhat similar rock-growing species, *H. pycnophylla* is also white-backed. Spread: (in gardens) 90cm (36in). Height: 38cm (15in).

Hosta ventricosa 'Aureomarginata'

Striking, large, spinach green hosta. Leaves: heart-shaped, deeply lobed, widely-veined, rippled at the edges and twisted slightly towards the tip, thin, glossy, the variegation starting yellow fading to cream. Flowers: late, bell-shaped, rich purple carried on straight leafy 90cm (36in) stems. Shade essential. The rare, slower-growing *H. ventricosa* var. *aureomaculata* has yellow to cream central variegation becoming green. Both are natural sports of the Chinese species, *H. ventricosa*. Spread: 120cm (48in). Height: 50cm (20in).

Hosta venusta

Miniature, green-leaved hosta species. Leaves: variably near oval, blade slightly wavy, smooth, matt, mid-green. Flowers: free-flowering racemes of funnel-shaped purple flowers at the tops of straight, bare, slender stems to 20cm (8in) in mid- to late summer. Useful in sinks and troughs, rock gardens and pots. Spread: 60cm (24in). Height: 10cm (4in).

'Veronica Lake'

Medium-sized, grey-green and yellow hosta. Leaves: heart-shaped with a thin powdery bloom, grey-green, margined yellow becoming cream, carried on exceptionally long leaf stalks. Flowers: mid-season, funnel-shaped, pale mauve, on straight, bare stems to 40cm (24in). Like its parent, *H.* 'Pearl Lake', it makes fast-growing, symmetrical mounds. When grown in full shade but good light, the leaf margins become chartreuse and the centres deep sea-green, a most attractive combination. Lovely in containers. Spread: 90cm (36in). Height: 40cm (16in).

Hosta *'Veronica Lake'* makes a rounded mound of delightful grey-green leaves margined yellowy cream in some sun, but more quietly coloured when grown in shade. Lovely in a container.

'Whirlwind'

Distinctive and colourful medium to large hosta, making an unruly mound. Leaves: oval to heart-shaped, deeply lobed, the blade twisted, pointed at the tip, conspicuously veined, ivory gradually turning chartreuse, then green, the wide irregular margin dark green. Flowers: mid- to late season, funnel-shaped, lavender, on straight, bare 60cm (24in) stems. The varying tonal blends of the variegation throughout the summer and the unruly upright habit make this a spectacular hosta. Spread: 90cm (36in). Height: 45cm (18in).

'Wide Brim'

Medium-sized, boldly variegated green and yellow hosta. Leaves: broadly heart-shaped, deeply lobed, slightly cupped and puckered, dark green, the yellow to cream variegation irregular, sometimes streaking into the green centre, the marginal colour varying with the density of the shade. Flowers: mid-season, funnel-shaped, pale mauve, on straight, bare stems to 60cm (24in). One of the loveliest and most useful of hostas, distinct in its appearance and excellent in pots and tubs, as well as in the garden and for flower arrangement. 'Stetson' is a sport having markedly upturned leaf blades. Spread: 90cm (36in). Height: 38cm (15in).

'Zounds'

Large, chartreuse to deep golden-yellow hosta. Leaves: round to heart-shaped, deeply lobed, folded into the navel, thick, wavy and slightly concave, conspicuously puckered, dark chartreuse to brassy gold, holding its colour well, even in deep shade. Flowers: mid-season, funnel-shaped, very pale lavender on straight, leafy stems to 60cm (24in). Slug and snail resistant. Spread: 120cm (48in). Height: 50cm (20in).

FURTHER INFORMATION

All postal addresses and telephone numbers mentioned are correct at the time of going to press.

Societies Specialising in Hostas

The British Hosta and Hemerocallis Society, Toft Monks, The Hithe, Rodborough Common, Stroud, Gloucestershire GL5 5BN; 01453 873 274; email: bhhs@classicfm.net

The American Hosta Society, 2489 Jack's View Court, Snellville, Georgia 30078-4178; (404) 713-3009; email: Hostanut@Bellsouth.net

Gardens to Visit (United Kingdom)

RHS Wisley, Woking, Surrey GU23 6QB

The Savill Garden, Windsor Great Park, Wick Lane, Englefield Green, Surrey TW20 0UU

Gardens To Visit (United States)

Dubuque Arboretum and Botanical Gardens, 3800 Arboretum Drive, Dubuque, Iowa, 52001

Longwood Gardens, Idea Garden, Kennett Square, Pennsylvania 19348

Minnesota Landscape Arboretum, Hosta Glade, 3675 Arboretum Drive, Chanhassen, Minnesota 55317

The Scott Arboretum of Swarthmore College, Hosta Garden and Terry Shane Teaching Garden, 500 College Avenue, Swarthmore, Pennsylvania 19081

Nurseries (United Kingdom)

Ann and Roger Bowden Hostas, Sticklepath, Okehampton, Devon EX20 2NL; 01837 840482;
email: bowdenhostas@eclipse.co.uk;
website: www.hostas-uk.com

Apple Court Garden and Nursery, Hordle Lane, Hordle, Lymington, Hampshire SO41 OHU; 01590 642130;
email: applecourt@btinternet.com;
website: www.applecourt.com

Goldbrook Plants, Hoxne, Eye, Suffolk IP21 5AN;
01379 668770

Merlin Hostas, Bicton, Shrewsbury, Shropshire SY3 8EF;
01743 850773 email: Jessica@MertonNursery.freeserve.co.uk

Park Green Nurseries, Wetheringsett, Stowmarket, Suffolk IP14 5QH; 01728 860139;
email: nurseries@parkgreen.fsnet.co.uk;
website: www. hostasonline.co.uk

Nurseries (United States)

Eagle Bay Hosta Gardens, 10749 Bennett Road, Dunkirk, NY 14048; (716) 366-8844

Green Hill Farm, Inc, P.O. Box 16306, Chapel Hill, NC 27516; (919) 383-4533

Hilltop Nursery, 3307 N State Hwy F, Ash Grove, MO 65604; (417) 672-2259

Naylor Creek Nursery, 2610 West Valley Road, Chimacum, WA 98325; (360) 732-4983

Plant Delights Nursery Inc, 9241 Sauls Road, Raleigh, NC 27603-9326; (919) 772-4794

Savory's Gardens Inc, 5300 Whiting Avenue, Edina, MN 55439-1249; (952) 941-8755

Wade and Gatton, 1288 Gatton Rocks Road, Belville, Ohio 44813-319; (419) 883-3191

Books

The Hosta Book, P. Aden (ed), (Batsford, 1992)
The Genus Hosta, W. G. Schmid, (Batsford, 1992)
Hostas, Diana Grenfell, (The Hardy Plant Society, 1993)

The Gardener's Guide to Growing Hostas, Diana Grenfell,
(David & Charles, 1996)
The Hosta Handbook, M. R. Zilis, (Q & Z Nursery, Inc.,
Rochelle, Illinois, 1999)
Bulletins of the British Hosta and Hemerocallis Society.
Bulletins of the American Hosta Society & The Hosta Journal
of The American Hosta Society.

Websites

British Hosta and Hemerocallis Society:
www.casaroccca.com/BHHS/html
American Hosta Society: www.hosta.org
Dutch Hosta Society: www.hostavereniging.nl

RHS Award of Garden Merit

The following hostas have been awarded the RHS Award
of Garden Merit:

Hosta 'Aureomarginata'
  (*ventricosa*)
H. 'Blue Angel' (*sieboldiana*)
H. crispula
H. fortunei var. *albopicta*
H. fortunei f. *aurea*
H fortunei var. *aureomarginata*
H. fortunei var. *hyacinthina*
H. 'Francee' (*fortunei*)
H. 'Frances Williams'
  (*sieboldiana*)
H. 'Golden Tiara'
H. 'Halcyon' (Tardiana
  Group)
H. 'Honeybells'
H. 'Krossa Regal'

H. lancifolia
H. 'Love Pat' (*tokudama*)
H. 'Paxton's Original'
  (*sieboldii*)
H. plantaginea var. *japonica*
H. 'Royal Standard'
H. 'Sagae'
H. 'Shade Fanfare'
H. sieboldiana var. *elegans*
H. 'Sum and Substance'
H. undulata var. *erromena*
H. undulata var. *undulata*
H. undulata var. *univittata*
H. ventricosa
H. venusta
H. 'Wide Brim'

INDEX

Acknowledgements

Illustrations: Patrick Mulrey
Copy-editor: Simon Maughan
RHS Editor: Barbara Haynes
Proofreader: Rae Spencer-Jones
Index: Dorothy Frame

The Publisher would like to thank
the following people for their kind
permission to reproduce their
photographs:

Garden Picture Library: 1 (Sunniva
Harte), 2 (Jerry Pavia), 15 (Howard
Rice), 19, 28 and 51 (Steven Wooster),
52 (Sunniva Harte), 55 (Geoff Dann),
58 (Juliette Wade).

Mike Shadrack (all other pages).

Jacket Image: Garden Picture Library
(Howard Rice).